SEEING THE *figure* NOW

AF334188

SEEING THE *figure* NOW

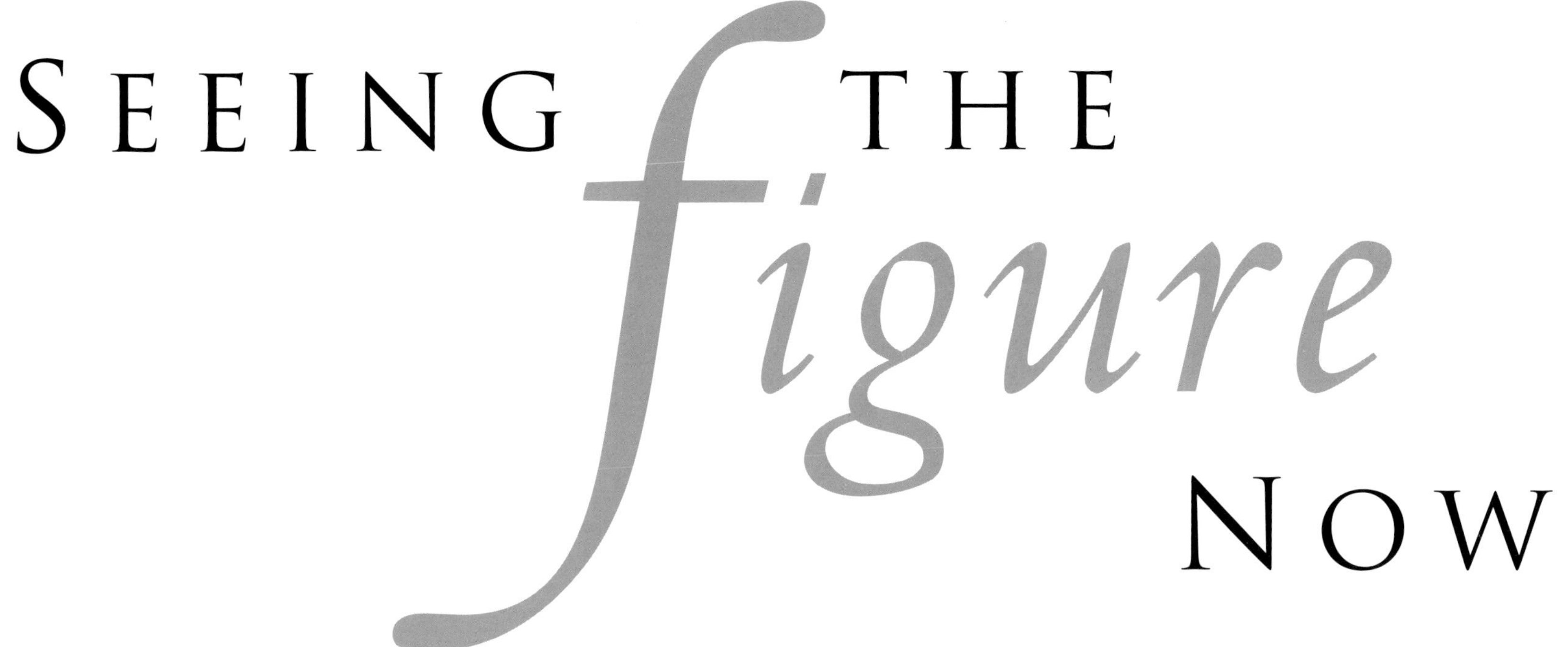

CURATED BY DENNIS ADRIAN

An exhibition organized by
The Betty Rymer Gallery of
The School of the Art Institute
of Chicago

20 October – 6 December 1995

TABLE OF CONTENTS

Copyright © 1995, The Betty Rymer Gallery
The School of the Art Institute of Chicago Press
All rights reserved.

Library of Congress Card No. 95-71873
ISBN 0-9637817-4-x

Design by Winge & Associates, Inc., Chicago, Illinois
Printed by Performance Graphics, Inc., Elmhurst, Illinois
Printing Arts Lithotech, Inc., Chicago, Illinois

Cover: Richard Willenbrink, *Orchidelirium*, 1993 (cat. no. 34)

ACKNOWLEDGMENTS

The initial concept for *Seeing the Figure Now* was presented by Dan Gustin to former Director of Exhibitions and Events at The School of the Art Institute, Joyce Fernandes. Through their perseverance and the curatorial and scholarly direction of art historian and critic Dennis Adrian, this project became a reality. We are particularly grateful to the participating artists Anne Abrons, Tim Doud, Dan Gustin, Mark Jackson, Robert Lucy, and Richard Willenbrink whose works reflect the resurgent interest in contemporary figurative painting.

It is with great thanks that we acknowledge the administrative support we have received from Dr. Carol Becker, Dean of Faculty/Interim President; Jana Wright, Special Assistant to the Dean; and Paul Elitzik, Director of Student Publications/ Faculty Publications Advisor. We are indebted as well to Dr. Paul Pribbenow, Vice President for Institutional Advancement, and his staff. Special acknowledgment is given to Claire Broadfoot, Assistant Director of the Betty Rymer Gallery, who provided invaluable assistance in administering the exhibition and catalogue. The coordination and installation of the exhibit was facilitated by the Betty Rymer Gallery staff: Edgar Bryan, Suzanne Dijak, Bob Dornberger, Matthew Flor, Matt Key, and Max Lesser.

Beyond The School of the Art Institute, several institutions and individuals have lent invaluable assistance. Foremost among them, the Illinois Arts Council, a state agency, provided partial funding for the exhibition. In Chicago, we thank Sonia Zaks, Sonia Zaks Gallery, for her professional guidance and Michael Tropea and Tom Van Eynde for their fine photography. We gratefully acknowledge the careful editing of this catalogue by Sue Taylor and its handsome design created by Robin Winge and her colleagues at Winge & Associates. Finally, our special thanks to the individuals and galleries who so generously lent artwork to the exhibition; without them this project could not have been realized.

Jeanne Long
Interim Director, Exhibitions and Events

SEEING THE FIGURE NOW:
Beyond the Metaphysical Mirror

"Seeing the Figure Now" is perhaps both too brief and too broad a title for this exhibition, which inevitably can deal only with some aspects of the wide and flourishing field of American figure painting today. Even just what is meant by the term "figure painting" is very likely not the same for everyone, and so it seems necessary to clarify this and several related points in order that the directions represented by the six artists in the present show can easily be grasped. The traditions and perspectives to which these artists are connected involve a number of commonalities. All but one of the artists work *primarily* from observation of the figure, although this practice is usually the basis for elements which are, for expressive and compositional considerations, invented or modified from the "seen." For those artists who frequently employ a good deal of other imagery—still life, interiors, and the like—in conjunction with the figure, it is in these aspects that invention may play a large part. Dan Gustin and Richard Willenbrink are good examples here, though this quality appears also in the others, especially Anne Abrons and Robert Lucy.

Most of the artists work within familiar categories—the nude, portrait, single freestanding figure (nude or not), self-portrait, invented subject, and the figure or figure group in an interior. These divisions have never been rigidly separated from one another, and it is typical of the artists here that such categories are combined or elided in various ways, producing interesting and unusual sub-types and hybrid forms. Perhaps most engaging among these are the nude self-portraits, also often single freestanding figures; this special type will be further considered below. Usually, these artists employ a life-size scale or close to it—now above, now below. A corollary is that their full-figure compositions reach the scale of monumental figure painting, one of the central categories of Western and (to a lesser degree) other artistic traditions since antiquity. It is probably not too much to say that this kind of painting is the major format of Western painting and has been so regarded, officially or unofficially, for many centuries. One could even argue that most significant developments in Western painting since the Renaissance have been either in relation or in reaction to it.

by Dennis Adrian

Then too, the six artists dealt with here all work in a painterly manner—what the Germans call *malerisch*. The brushstrokes are perceptible and frequently organized into compositional ensembles along with or in spite of their "descriptive" functions. There is impasto; the energies and directions of the artists' hands are visible, are meant to be savored as pure painting, and can function as vital formal elements in the whole composition. Paint is manipulated with sensuosity and vigor, but these gestural aspects of the paint handling do not disrupt spatial constructs or the solidity of forms. On the contrary, form and space are animated and energized by this kind of brushwork, which is often combined with passages of different and quieter tempi. All these considerations are pursued in the aim of an expressive intensity of feeling.

For each of our artists, drawing plays an extremely important role, a little different in each case. They all draw quite a bit from life, exploring compositional possibilities, creating loose organizational rehearsals for painted works or, less often, studies of particular aspects of a given composition, usually concerning individual figure placement (as in the case of Willenbrink). Drawings in liquid or colored media—watercolor, gouache, pastel, colored pencil—may have a direct technical connection with issues of painting, but none of our artists, with rare exceptions, seems to do carefully realized drawings that are full studies for paintings: the primary function of drawing for them is to gain a secure control over form and an ability to realize it with conviction, *whether the form is observed or invented*. Clearly, painting for these artists must retain a good deal of spontaneity and discovery in its processes. It would never do for them to follow in a painting an idea fully planned out in meticulous compositional studies, thereby giving drawing too restrictive a role in the reactive and inventive painting procedures which are paramount for them.

A significant current among our artists is their involvement with metaphysical content in all their work. This means that metaphysical considerations occur in contexts other than invented subjects, fantasies, symbolic representations, themes relating to some text or other, myths, legends, and the like. This is an aspect of art described only with difficulty since it involves the interplay of states of feeling which are not easily conceptualized and which might in fact be possible to know only through experience. It is related to the mechanisms of visual perception and its interpretations, particularly in allowing the recognition of forms or images other than purely functional ones. Perhaps we are most accustomed to encountering this experience in works of the *Scuola Metafisica*, Dada, and Surrealism, where very frequently familiar objects come together in the most surprisingly unexpected conjunctions. While we might easily identify every object in, say, a de Chirico painting, it is not at all clear what they are doing there together. Because the ensemble lacks, in ordinary terms, any obvious functional interconnections, we examine each element carefully and again and again to assure ourselves that we have not made a mistake of recognition somewhere along the line which is preventing us from grasping the expected functional natures and relationships of the objects depicted. This intense scrutiny and re-examination of the forms and images contribute to our achieving a much deeper awareness of them (and their unconscious associative possibilities) than we customarily experience in ordinary seeing.

Usually, we look at something only thoroughly enough to satisfy ourselves that we know what it is (what it is for or might do) and what response, if any, we intend to make in regard to it. When we look further, beyond those aspects that provide us with a serviceable functional recognition of the object or image, we can begin to apprehend its many other qualities—its structure, its resemblance, actual or imagined, to other objects and images—and we thereby set into play a whole series of associations which the object, its image, form, or referential potential might have for us separately. This enhanced kind of perception is what is sometimes called "poetic awareness"; it is the credible world of knowledge and emotional affect that is the nature of artistic experience itself and that extends and deepens our understanding of the world and our own existence. Because this esthetic territory is not entirely subject to rational considerations, it is often described as visionary or even mystical. Whether or not this is so, esthetic experience does seem to resemble the states of spiritual coherence and unity of all existence with which many spiritual disciplines are concerned. For these reasons, art can be described not only as an aspect of existence but as an important and revealing way of experiencing it.

This function of art may often involve reversals of the ordinary and realizations not altogether comfortable. Marcel Duchamp's *Fountain* (1917), a porcelain urinal placed on its back on a pedestal as a sculpture, provides a still shocking interplay of sensations as we recognize the object functionally, check our interpretation to determine that we are not mistaken in this identification, and in doing so come to an experience of the object as a sculptural form of great interest in itself apart from and in spite of its usual function. Duchamp goes further to propose a new function (fountain), which is a reversal of the usual one. A critical feature of Duchamp's accomplishment is to call attention to the fact that ordinary things, even those which have presumably come into being for some specific mundane purpose, may be perceived in completely different and hitherto unexpected aspects.

Each of our artists displays a very challenging concern with new ways to experience various categories of pictorial type and artistic invention. In a sense, the Duchampian method is turned upon art itself, again, with precedents in Duchamp and in Francis Picabia. The works in this exhibition can thus be seen not only as a continuation of certain well-established kinds and functions of painting but also as a refreshing enlargement of our notions of these modes and traditions. Therefore, just as Goya's paintings enliven and advance our experience of Tiepolo, as Velázquez does for Titian, Rembrandt for Caravaggio, Rubens for Veronese, and Manet for this entire tradition, our artists are connected with it largely through the early modernist example of Manet and others, particularly Courbet and Degas.

THE GRAND MANNER

The preceding observations indicate that the artists we are concerned with continue to develop what is often called the Grand Manner or the Grand Style, a concept most familiar from Sir Joshua Reynolds' *Discourses on Art* (1769-90). This grand tradition is often seen as originating in Titian, Veronese, Giorgione, and Venetian painting of the fifteenth and sixteenth centuries in general. Although Venetian painting itself owes a good deal to Raphael, Michelangelo, and even Leonardo, the energized brushwork characteristic of the Grand Manner is a specifically Venetian contribution, exemplified wonderfully in the mature Titian and in Tintoretto. With an important impetus provided by Caravaggio, this

manner continues through the Baroque in Guido Reni, Pietro da Cortona, Poussin, Rubens, Van Dyck, Velázquez, Rembrandt and Hals, Fragonard, Boucher, Tiepolo, Goya, and to Courbet, Manet, and Degas at one of the crucial points of the emergence of modernism. Manet's sly and knowing references to Titian, Giorgione, and Raphael, perceptible to many of his contemporaries, in *Luncheon on the Grass* and *Olympia* (both 1863) are perhaps the best-known demonstrations of this linkage of modern painting and the grand tradition. The twentieth century is replete with examples of this sort, particularly in the careers of Picasso, Matisse, and such overlooked figures as the great German painter, draftsman, and printmaker, Lovis Corinth. In his idiosyncratic way, Max Beckmann can also be related to these concerns, as can, more recently, somewhat outré figures such as Balthus.

SOME CRITICAL ISSUES IN
FIGURE PAINTING

While many recent examples of the tendencies under discussion can be adduced from the very rich field of twentieth-century art, it is worth mentioning a number of artists who seem especially relevant. Each has achieved a hard-won eminence in the overall climate of contemporary painting, which, by and large, appears dedicated to abstraction or to currents derived from (deliberately) restricted aspects of Expressionism, German and other. The relevant figure painters are Robert Barnes, Jack Beal, Lucian Freud,

Paul Georges, Alfred Leslie, and, in a more limited fashion, James McGarrell, Alice Neel, Philip Pearlstein, and Sylvia Sleigh. Among these, Barnes and McGarrell seem more closely concerned with pictorial invention, fantasy and imagination, and complex metaphysical vision than do the others, but this is a matter of degree rather than kind. One can easily find similarities among Gustin, Barnes, and McGarrell, between Willenbrink and Georges, Sleigh and Lucy, but the perhaps more "observational" tendencies of Freud, Leslie, Neel, Pearlstein, and Sleigh appear as well. Mark Jackson recalls aspects of Manet and Beckmann at the same time, and Tim Doud's nudes and their coloration are occasionally reminiscent of Pearlstein.

A vexing question for many regarding figure painting and whatever is considered realism is the relation of the painter's construct to the "seen." The long tradition of fidelity to optical data is itself a confusing set of issues, all arising out of different notions of what "optical fidelity" is, what the "seen" is, and even of what *seeing* is. And these points are inextricably tangled with the understanding of perception, its very methods and mechanisms, the nature of memory, seeing, and knowing, and more. Therefore, it must be emphasized that our six painters are *not* primarily concerned with presenting some uninflected two-dimensional transposition of the "seen," although in the works of each we see, largely because of the perceptual training of our own cultural conventions, many things that we would say "look like that." Whether or not this is or even can be so is an enormously complicated question which cannot be settled here, but perhaps some useful remarks bearing on the issues are possible.

Rather than presenting the "seen," or even what the camera, film, or video might be said to see or at least *to show*, our artists aim at presenting a vision which the eye and mind can accept as a (complex) visual entity with its own powerful reality. The painting will be convincing even if the subject, the "scene," is something we know is impossible or at least highly unlikely as an empirical aspect of ordinary experience, and even if it violates that "reality" upon which we rely to negotiate our way through the world as delivered by our senses and their related interpretive mechanisms and processes. This situation is not easily discussed in detail, but examples of such convincing vision can be offered. For instance, we can find persuasive and visually consistent paintings of miracles and events of religious history, legends, and fables even when we may feel that such an event never occurred or that if it did, it never looked like that, and so forth. The phenomenon is perhaps related to "suspension of disbelief," although in successful painting of this kind, we do not have to make any effort to accept "the impossible" as actual in some important way. This is what is also called the poetic dimension in some contexts.

A familiar example occurs in Manet's wonderful *Bar at the Folies-Bergère* (1883), where the reflection in the mirror behind the bar cannot be made to agree with the objects in front of the mirror and which ought to be reflected in it. While we find Manet's vision completely convincing to our mind and eye (if, in this case, there is any meaningful separation of their functions), it is not possible, employing models and props, to construct a set-up that corresponds visually to Manet's "scene." Just how this is achieved is difficult to say; one modernist approach has been to point out that Manet's painting has an architecture, a structure (the *composition* in one important sense) which is itself satisfying and harmonious and may be apprehended apart from the descriptive (realist?) elements of the painting. Perhaps this is so, at least in some ways, but it is difficult to imagine the viewer who would grasp this structure *before and independently* of Manet's scene. Such a viewer would have to be completely innocent of the interpretations of perception and visual systems of Western (and much other) art. It is the Wild-Child problem: how can one obtain this primal innocence of seeing? Is there such a thing? Advances into the mechanisms of perception on the neurological and electrochemical levels will tell us much more about these things, but at present they remain largely mysterious and the subject of many conflicting but equally attractive hypotheses.

Another relevant aspect of Manet's work is the way he employs and refreshes established visual systems in painting—tonal modeling, color not greatly at odds with what we expect from our functional identification of the forms, acceptable scale relationships among parts of the whole, varying degrees of clarity in different portions, and manipulation of light in ways that confirm our understanding of the entire image. These qualities are not necessarily closely tied to the notion of "optical fidelity" in its usual meaning, i.e., this is the way and the only way these things *could* look in this situation and under these conditions. Though there are serious difficulties with this very idea, as has already been noted, it is one that still has currency. Manet's genius is able to play upon visual systems and perceptual *affects* which are part of our ordinary paraphernalia for interpreting experience in such a way as to engage fully our sense of the convincing while also creating a sense of special, enhanced vision (and understanding and feeling) which we can regard as his perception brought to life in us. Idiosyncracies of color handling, rhythm and energy of the brush, idiosyncratic forms, and numerous other elements provide us with a personal and individual *experience* of Manet's vision and feeling, whether or not he was consciously aware of them. This is the sense of life of the painting: whether or not any plant, person, or animal in the image is understood as alive, we experience a vitality which extends or connects to our own, sometimes leading us to unprecedented levels of existential awareness. This is what occurs when we feel enriched, moved, or changed by a work of art: we have achieved a more profound grasp of the nature of the world and our experience of it than before.

In the context of this kind of experience, it is often a pleasure to find that when upon close examination we discover in the painting something that is not "possible," this realization does not disrupt but may even enhance the sense of conviction possessed by the whole work. Some artists, such as Corinth, have spoken of this as a "visionary" aspect of art and there is indeed often something rather strange about it, even eerie. This unaccountable strangeness occasionally pervading the ordinary is the specialty of artists such as James Ensor, in what at first sight might seem ordinary or even conventional figure or still-life paintings, and in such marvels as Velázquez's *bodegónes*, where the numinous pervades the elements of daily life in a most remarkable way. Chardin can do it with a few plums or Manet with a single tangerine or stalk of asparagus. The effect here is not realism (at least of the ordinary kind) but of truth. Our response to what we see, how we see it, and what awareness is created in us is: *Yes!*

SOME SIGNIFICANT THEMES OF FIGURE PAINTING

Each of the artists in the present exhibition demonstrates this ability to construct a vision which, however invented and inventive, offers a satisfying convincingness, created and enriched with varying factors such as color, handling, emotional tone, spatial structure, all elements important in putting forth the unmistakable experience of a particular sensibility. This sensibility or temperament defines the characteristic personality of each artist and his or her work; it also determines the insight, meaning, and, in the deepest and fullest sense, artistic content of the work. From this circumstance, we can begin to examine how different artists approach similar issues, themes, subjects, and the sorts of (mixed) categories of painting touched upon above. The

principal categories for our purposes are the nude, self-portrait, portrait, and metaphysical subject. Again, these are not mutually exclusive divisions: they overlap, and in this overlapping some of the most striking and revealing artistic statements are made, directly articulating the spirit of the work.

The centrality of the nude to the traditions with which our artists are connected can scarcely be exaggerated. The study and evolution of the nude in Western art since antiquity is an aspect of an intellectual development having to do with a fuller comprehension of the physical world not only through the advances in physics of Galileo and others but also through the greater knowledge of human anatomy gained by physicians, natural scientists, and artists such as Leonardo. The understanding of the body as a physical mechanism and an organic structure united the awareness of what it is to be human with the rest of natural creation: man and the universe are seen as subject to the same laws of physics or dictates of creation.

The identification of an image as a human form involves the supposition of an identity of potential specificity to the "being" so identified. Whenever we see an image we read as a figure (or even part of one), we try to determine not just what but also *who* it might be or represent. This imputation of identity involves the imagining of a personality and its emotional states; that is, what might this creature's attitude be toward us and what is ours to it? These are psychological issues tied up with the complex nature of perception and our awareness of it. When the human image is given particulars as to size, gender, age, position, and facial expression, we have moved closer to the idea of the portrait in its usual sense, where the specific and delimiting physical idiosyncrasies of the subject play important roles, and our apprehension of feeling, character, attitude, and emotion associated with the image *and* its subject becomes very complicated. This reaction to the portrait and to the sense of the animate presence there also is affected by our voyeuristic security: no matter how intimidating the portrait might seem, we can examine it safely in the knowledge that it cannot respond and that it must submit to our examination for as long as we like. Because of this, the psychological experience of a portrait image allows us a depth, range, and freedom of interpretation which might be difficult or impossible to carry out in the presence of the person him- or herself.

The self-portrait brings further intensities to all the aspects of the human image and the portrait sketched above, at least in those instances where the self-portrait involves a physical likeness rather than a symbolic or synecdochic representation. The principal reason for this is that the voyeuristic privacy of experiencing the image is broken in a special way *during its creation*, when the artist and the viewer are "the same person," or at least the persona of the artist exists in two separate but simultaneous aspects, creator and viewer. Opportunities for psychological probing and revelation are even greater than in the portrait of another person, and there is a correspondingly greater intricacy to the conscious and unconscious processes of editing or inflecting the image

of the self this way or that, for one reason or another (or many). When the self-portrait is of the entire figure, additional expressive possibilities of pose, gesture, costume, and setting can come into play to a greater degree than in the partial figure, but not too much greater than their functions in any full-length portrait.

When there is a conflation of the types of the portrait, self-portrait, and *the nude*, the situation is greatly enhanced in expressive and analytical scope. The self-analyses and revelations of the ordinary self-portrait are joined to the consideration of the entire exposed physical nature of the subject as an expressive likeness. Many interesting questions arise: why has the artist chosen to show him- or herself unclothed? Reasons such as the unavailability of nude models, warm weather, and so forth are very limited and unsatisfying. Such an exposure always has the element of confrontation (here of both self and viewer) bound up in it, and the very significant erotic, or at least libidinal, potential of perhaps any figurative image will inevitably play a large part. These factors can become powerfully interactive when we feel that the body is shown us without significant idealization or "improvements," that is, when the figurative image is a portrait of the whole body, not simply a likeness head stuck on a generalized or stereotypical somatic image.

The history of the nude self-portrait image is curious. One important point of origin is a magical pen-and-brush drawing (1503) by Albrecht Dürer, in which his penetrating gaze and concentrated facial expression are more than matched by the ruthless presentation of his knottily muscled, wiry body, where each part, including the genitals, is delineated with great particularity. The exact purpose of this drawing is not fully determined, although it very likely involves the study of a figure for some other work, a painting or print. But as Dürer would not seem to have had any trouble procuring the usual sort of model, why did he use himself? Why is it so relentlessly the portrait of the whole body rather than just the creation of the figure pose and type the artist might have required for another purpose? Why did he not *invent* such a figure? These are all tantalizing mysteries, and many of the same questions come to mind about most subsequent nude self-portraits since, in a very profound and focused way, they are intensely self-reflective productions which are also meant to be experienced by others.

Creating the nude self-portrait image is also an intricate affair psychologically because each of us (including artists) has multiple visual and other notions about the self. Some of these are greatly at variance with one another and must be rectified, accommodated, harmonized, and/or contrasted in the image. For example, each of us has an image of how he or she looks which is gained from the mirror. But this image is both in reverse and the wrong size, since a reflected image appears to be twice as far from the viewer as he or she is from the mirror. In addition to this mirror image, there are the images of what we *imagine* we look like, what we *want* to look like, how we *feel*, and how we *believe* we appear in other kinds of images such as art, photography, video, or film. All of these images inevitably play some part in the creation of the nude or any self-portrait.

Since Dürer's remarkable drawing in the early sixteenth century, nude self-portraits are extremely rare—if they exist at all—until the later nineteenth century. Edvard Munch did a fascinating nude *half-length* self-portrait in 1895, and Corinth produced some nude self-portrait drawings (seated in the studio) around 1908, when he also did some nearly nude character self-portraits (as Bacchus) which, like the Munch of more than a decade before, are half-length figures. Before his death in 1918, Egon Schiele did quite a few nude self-portraits of the entire figure in drawings and gouaches. The German painter Paula Modersohn-Becker, just after the turn of the century, did several nude self-portraits, at least one full length, usually with suggestions of a goddesslike character made through accessories such as jewelry or flowers. It is of the greatest interest and importance that a woman artist made the first significant pictures of this kind in the present century.

Modersohn-Becker's heirs in this line of painting are themselves notable, the two most prominent being Neel and Sleigh. Neel's fearless late portrait (1980) of her aged and collapsing physique is both moving and lovable; she shows herself with the most remarkable aplomb rather than bravado, and the result compels respect. Sleigh's images of her nude self usually frankly acknowledge the existence of the painter's mirror. In *Self-Portrait with Blue Dress* (1970), her nude image appears *only* in the mirror behind her painted image in the blue dress—a perfect example of the mysterious image we find both physically impossible and utterly convincing. In this painting, Sleigh introduces herself (or her image, or her reflection of and upon herself) as her own muse, a figure that exists in a doubly fictive metaphysical territory, the painted image of the reflected space. The awareness of a self-reliant feminist sensibility is admirably put forth here.

The nude self-portraits of Abrons, Lucy, and Willenbrink owe something to these women and to other artists, such as Paul Georges, whose nude self-portraits are among the most important and least-known accomplishments of modern American painting. William Beckman's and Gregory Gillespie's nude self-portraits, on the other hand, belong to a somewhat different painting tradition, that of precisely finished, enamellike surfaces, almost invisible brushwork, and highly realized detail: this is perhaps more the "optical fidelity" tradition, which of course also has roots in Dürer. The nude self-portraits in the present show are of several differing and interesting types: Abrons takes pains to inform us that her identity as an artist involves an uncompromising acceptance of the self, physical and mental, a touchstone of honesty and truth in her art. This is not to say that she avoids invention or that she does not formulate the image in response to a whole variety of personal and esthetic concerns but that the expression of these things must be convincing and present some aspect of truth as a metaphysical goal. In this quest, her nude self-portraits and other portraits invariably set forth remarkably keen and sometimes uncomfortable states of feeling.

Lucy's large *Artist and Models* (1993, cat. no. 25) picks up an aspect of Sleigh's *Self-Portrait in a Blue Dress*: the nude self-portrait is very clearly the image reflected in the mirror. Lucy extends this idea ingeniously by having the mirror on an easel, thereby tying together the mirror-painting-reflection problems. In front of this easel is a still-life arrangement of the painter's clothes, objects which both have and disclose his shape in yet another way. Not only are they slack, empty, and soft but are also foreshortened and overlapped in the total image, becoming metaphorical transpositions of the artist's "form" and identity. Just behind and to the left of the mirror on the easel, we see a large painting resting on the floor; this image is of a triple female nude, three views of the same model. The painting is "by" Sleigh, establishing Lucy's picture as an homage to Sleigh among its other functions. The triple nude inevitably suggests the three graces and their role in artistic theory and metaphysics, especially their traditional activities of giving, receiving, and returning. Here, these are presented as the functions of art and of the artist. The lingerie display form in *Artist and Models*, the hand, mask, hat, and the portion of a figure painting reflected in the mirror— all speak of Lucy's awareness of the nature of images, especially figurative ones, which can so easily illuminate aspects of the human condition. His painting thus shows us in more than one way "*how* he looks" and also at what he looks, and reveals much about his notions of the artist's role.

Willenbrink's *Nude Self-Portrait* (1995, cat. no. 35) takes yet another line in the consideration of the artist's image. His figure is placed in a manner recalling the idealized (but with strangely individualized facial features) figure of Leonardo's *Vitruvian Man* (c. 1490), a prime Renaissance example of the understanding of the relationship of the human body to underlying or subsuming structural principles governing the universe at large. Willenbrink's somewhat ironic contrast of his own all-too-irregular and idiosyncratic physical form to Leonardo's ideal trenchantly investigates the relationship of specific and actual forms to generalized and constructed (Platonic) ones. The somewhat *sfumato* effects of modeling in the body and to suggest the body hair are a kind of twist on Leonardo's smoky tonalism. In Willenbrink's picture, moreover, the figure is set against a loose, painterly background of crackling energy and vigor, recalling similar features in Corinth's figure and portrait paintings.

The nude proper is naturally an adjunct or perhaps rather the source of the nude self-portrait, and it is accordingly a fundamental category in the works of each of our artists. The nude itself is not such a clearly defined category as we might think. Is a figure with a small amount of drapery or with accessories a nude? Are images of the crucified Christ wearing but a loincloth "nudes"? The distinctions Sir Kenneth Clark makes between nude and naked are relevant here and are useful in evaluating each figural image on its own merits. Several works in the exhibition play with these ambiguities or multivalent possibilities of the nude. Abrons' *Ken in Gay Pride Parade Costume* (1994, cat. no. 6), for example, brings together several figure painting concepts. It is a single free-standing figure, it is a portrait—and one of a special type, the character portrait in which the sitter has a good deal to do with the persona presented. And since this figure has very little clothing (panties, shoes, and a wig), it is a kind of nude. What is unusual is that we are given not only the painter's reading of the person and his personality, but the painter's take on the sitter's view of aspects of his identity he wishes to put forth, or at least let us see. In this case, the sitter's interests are tied up with societal and even political issues, matters of public debate as well as individual conviction and commitment. The image he has chosen is deliberately provocative, and while not so unusual as to be unprecedented in our experience, might well be startling to many.

Because the costume elements involve transvestism as well as the general issue of costume (as opposed to ordinary apparel), the painting has a connection with the theatrical portrait, the character portrait *par excellence*. In that well-known kind of painting, we see an *artist*, assuming the appearance and identity of a character which, whether historical or not, is itself a compound artistic invention, created by the author (composer, librettist, choreographer), the actor (dancer, singer), and the painter. In front of Abrons' painting, we must ask: Just what kind of identity is being presented? Is the sitter's get-up meant to represent some specific person, type of person, temperament, or character, or is he showing us an invention, discovery, or revelation about his own nature? Are these two considerations mutually exclusive? They seem not to be in the usual theatrical portrait in which we are most often given a blend of the role or characterization that is the ostensible subject, the "subject of the *subject*" (the sitter) and of the character and persona of the sitter him- or herself.

Another extension of the basic idea of the nude is offered in Tim Doud's paintings, in which figures are presented in settings that might be the studio or might not. Doud shows us something that might be the life-class set-up with the nude model (seen from quite close) or could equally well be a more intimate study of someone he knows, whose character and personality are suggested somewhat by the elements of pose, facial expression, and the like. Because the figures are nude, possible erotic aspects of the relationship between model and artist (and viewer) are introduced, but not followed up. The result is a kind of reticence and privacy oddly combined with a high degree of intimacy. Doud's often cool palette and his way of interrupting his figures by the edge of the canvas bring to mind similar properties in the work of Pearlstein, especially up to 1980 (after which *his* palette is warmer). This cool coloration provides an emotional distance, and it is clear that in both Doud and Pearlstein these chromatic arrangements are deliberate expositions of color composition. Each artist is not merely putting down what is there to be seen, but has evolved pictorial constructs which, while not completely independent of the subject, may be appreciated to some degree on their own.

Doud's curious guarded intimacy (public privacy?)

differs from the affect of Pearlstein's pictures in many ways. The older artist takes pains to keep our realization of the body close to that we have about still-life objects: the inert figures seem so withdrawn that we feel they are not aware of us, the painter, or sometimes even of one another. Usually, the models' heads are truncated by the painting edge, their faces averted, their eyes closed, their features relaxed; their permanent immobility gives us the impression that we could never rouse them. In addition, the scale of Pearlstein's figures is often considerably over life size (or what we think of as life size). This scale monumentalizes the figures so that we are reminded of their nature as images—they are too big to *be* people—and while this gigantism can be a bit intimidating, it also establishes a psychic remove from the figures as living beings like us. This distancing encourages us to look at Pearlstein's paintings formally, to apprehend their ingenious compositions (often involving mirror images) and to keep us seeing his paintings *as painting*.

Pearlstein seems either to suppress a certain amount of detail, especially body hair, on the surfaces of his figures or to choose models who are relatively smooth-bodied. Whatever the case, our apprehension of his figures is sculptural more than specifically physical, and this further blunts the mechanisms which lead us to try to establish our "relationship" to the figure *as a person*. Pearlstein does not idealize the facial features of his models; they are recognizable from one painting to another. But, despite this likeness, the paintings are not quite portraits in the usual sense because our avenues of affect with the model are so obstructed. Pearlstein does do portraits, although with one possible exception (a commission) he has not done nude portraits. In his portraits, the monumental beings are alive and alert, and the scale given them by the artist imparts an imposing grandeur that is very interestingly set off against the greatly magnified particulars of their features. The sitters become iconic without losing their individuality; the result is a bit like the effects of later Roman colossal portrait sculpture, something explored in a very different way in the paintings of Leon Golub, also an occasional portraitist.

By contrast, Doud's use of smaller scale (sometimes noticeably *under* life size) and his attention to physical occurrences on the body's surface such as hair and coloration set his own emotional tone. His models also are recognizable, but their expressions do not remove them from the range of our (or the artist's) emotional affect. While the compositions are careful, the poses might be natural; we feel we might have just come upon someone we know asleep or resting unclothed. The parts of furniture which often interrupt our view of the figure also can suggest that we are sitting down observing the figure, perhaps waiting for a friend to wake from a nap. This intimism often contrasts strongly with Doud's chilly palette, and this chromatic manipulation as much as anything else prevents the intimacy from becoming more personal. The model remains private.

Doud's portraiture and self-portraiture also have something of this impersonal intimacy about them. The portrait of *Bishop Frank Griswold* (1994-95, cat. no. 11) presents some issues similar to those in Abrons' *Ken in Gay Pride Parade Costume*. The bishop wears episcopal robes and so is seen in his professional identity. But in this case we must not assume that the sitter is creating a character for us (although the artist might be). Bishop Griswold's professional and personal identities are melded in his vocation, his spiritual calling. He *is* a bishop, not dressing up as one, and he is a bishop all the time, not merely while at work. "Bishopness" is part of his personality and character (and vice versa) and is not easily separated from him in his other aspects as a human being. In this way, Bishop Griswold is like an artist whose identity, if it is authentic, should not be something that is turned on and off or only operates part of the time. An artist, too, has a vocation and in many ways it is or ought to be a spiritual one. In this connection, it is interesting to recall that Pearlstein has done a major ecclesiastical portrait also, of the primate of Philadelphia, and that Willenbrink has done a double portrait of a Lutheran minister and his wife. It would be informative to see all of these paintings side by side.

Behind both Doud's and Pearlstein's approaches to the nude and to the portrait is the curious example of Stanley Spencer. The English painter's unforgettable nudes of himself and his mistress done in the 1930s give us a proto-Pearlsteinian closeness of view and monumental scale, but it is combined with a careful lingering over a multitude of minute features on the surface of the body—not only hair but also tiny folds, imperfections, curious accidents of natural form, follicles, and textures which add up to a hallucinatory physical presence. Since the relationship between Spencer and his nude female companion is a personal one, it is the subject and reason for these paintings in a way which Pearlstein's never seem to be and which Doud's only equivocally suggest. Sleigh's group nudes do not enter into this personal territory either. Compositional necessities together with her interests in the personal and professional identities of her models are foremost—not a revealingly personal intimacy. This is reserved for portraits, nude and otherwise, of her husband, Lawrence Alloway, but even in two of the most important examples of these, *The Court of Pan* (after Signorelli) and *The Turkish Bath* (both 1973), the figures are disposed in an easy familiarity with one another (and the viewer) rather than projecting a personal intimacy.

These questions of intimacy and psychic remove are very much at the heart of Freud's figure painting over the past twenty years as well. His involvement with character and projections of feeling are notable in the way he juxtaposes several figures in the studio and especially in the telling contrasts and comparisons he presents between nude and clothed figures which, although they often have a near-Pearlsteinian remove to inner awareness and unresponsive repose, may at the same time be in physical contact with each other in such a way as to suggest some relationship between them. There is always a strong libidinal quotient in these possibilities which Freud does nothing to suppress (or specify).

It is worth pointing out that Freud's succulent, brushy surfaces and skillful variety of paint handling in this period connects him directly with the *malerisch* tradition of the Grand Manner and of our artists. In addition, he has from time to time created variations on such pictures from the past—his group portrait after Watteau, for example. Then too, his hanging of several of his own recent works at the Dulwich College Picture Gallery in conjunction with masterpieces from the museum's collection by Rubens, Van Dyck, and other grand-manner artists reveals his identification, emulation, and perhaps even ambitious competition with them.

Also in many of these recent paintings, Freud has explored unconventional aspects of the nude in his use of models whose physical proportions and somatic types are in strong contrast to the idealized, classically based, and stereotypical notions of the "beautiful nude" offered as a distillation or formulated construct of physical beauty. There is an irony in Freud's employment of very heavy models or such impressively massive physiques as that of the late performance artist Leigh Bowery. By emphasizing these somewhat unexpected physical types, Freud calls attention to similar figures in such grand-manner painters as Rubens, Jordaens, Rembrandt, Courbet, and, more recently, artists such as Corinth, Neel, and Ed Paschke. In the cases of the older artists (including Corinth), these figures usually derive from myth—nymphs, sileni, Bacchuses—or, in the case of Rembrandt, represent biblical figures such as Susannah. Past practice did not always adhere to norms of classical figure types but frequently responded to the variety of actual bodily variations, and in this way humanized figures of exalted status. Freud is perhaps doing the reverse, finding nobility, grandeur, and imposing dignity in the fleshy presence of ordinary people, or in figures such as Bowery whose ponderous bulk did not prevent his use of the body as his medium—in fact, his unforgettable appearance seems to have enhanced his artistic presence.

There is some of this exploration of the somatically atypical in our six artists as well: often this is a matter of costume (or lack of it) together with poses having a referential connection with these issues of body type. Abrons' *Ken in Gay Pride Parade Costume* and Willenbrink's *Nude Self-Portrait* certainly do so, and it might be said that all of Jackson's figure types are chosen or presented in such a way as to underline their departures from any classical canon while at the same time alluding to it in the postures and views he selects. Also, Abrons' portrait *Annette Maryan in My Studio* (1990, cat. no. 1) makes a supremely interesting and penetrating analysis of character and state of mind through her responses to the uniqueness of the sitter's striking physical appearance and pose.

Lucy's nudes, portraits, and other figures also have curious interplays among their categories, as in the *Reclining Nude with Flowers* (1992, cat. no. 24), which appears to be as much a portrait as a nude study: the provocative variety and arrangement of still-life elements in this picture suggest hermetic meanings and private associations—a metaphysical content, in fact. While all these objects may be regarded simply as studio props which enrich the whole vision, the *cartellino* on the wall behind the figure, the frank interestedness of her expression, and the bit of jewelry around the neck bring us close to if not into the realm of personal acquaintance. Perhaps the effect is like that of some of Gauguin's South Sea nudes, where one feels that the artist has gone beyond a forthright study of the model and has entered into the realm of feeling, attitude, and personal emotion for both artist and sitter. Lucy's other nude here, *The Mesmerist* (1994, cat. no. 28), brings off a similar effect with even more limited means: the tense pose of the model, her penetrating gaze, and the mysterious device (unplugged) on the wall behind her summon up an identity, a personality which goes beyond a purely formal regard of the nude figure, if there can be such a thing.

Metaphysical concerns are the point: is the sitter the mesmerist and if so, has she mesmerized us or the artist by her gaze, her nude figure, or the device on the wall? Is it *she* who is mesmerized? Or, are we to see the artist as mesmerist, who by special powers brings out things his subjects are not aware of or would not necessarily reveal except under his spell? Something of this out-of-the-ordinary feeling appears as well in Lucy's *Laura with Hats* (1993, cat. no. 26), where again the accessories—a skull, mask, wig form, sculptured head, painting, and various hats—all work together to emit a sense of a number of possible interrelated identities, each a bit sinister and extremely compelling. The magic of the ordinary or slightly strange that becomes so intense in this picture seems a direct connection with the attractively creepy moods of James Ensor's paintings of masks, hats, props, and model.

Lucy's portraits proper, such as *Stephanie D'Alessandro and David Rownd* (1993, cat. no. 27), announce themselves as portraits through the poses as much as composition. In this painting, we see from the way the figures are nestled together that their connection is an intimate one (engagement to be married) and that the presentation of this relationship is one of the principal functions of the painting. The couple seems at home, they are lounging on a "love seat," and their expressions seem at least to tolerate if not welcome our gaze. These are conventions of the familiar betrothal portrait, but the complexities of the still-life selection on the table before the couple, the reproduction of a George Grosz drawing pinned to the wall, and the spring landscape visible at the upper left manage, perhaps through the ingenuity of their arrangement and interesting color composition, to suggest a level of significance beyond incidental objects in a sitting room. The objects set up an allusive climate which has to do with the identities of the sitters, their interests or personalities, and this expressive task is carried out as much by an Ensorian ability to elicit the peculiarity of the ordinary as through any conventional kind of symbolism—of flowers, for example.

If the D'Alessandro-Rownd picture is a kind of metaphysical painting masquerading as a portrait, *Reclining Nude with Flowers* is a kind of portrait masquerading as a metaphys-ical nude. Such inventive inflections of pictorial categories often lend Lucy's paintings an appealing strangeness as our awareness fixes now on one, now on another of the varieties of artistic situations offered us in a single work. This unexpected blending of pictorial types also infuses Abrons' portraits. *Family Portrait* (1993, cat. no. 4) mixes her children's portraits with her self-portrait and an image of her husband, the painter David Sharpe, who is here seen taking a photograph not, apparently, of his wife and children but of the *mirror* Abrons has required to make her painting or, alternatively, of the painting itself. Furthermore, in the background next to the figure of Sharpe is a rendering of *one of his figure paintings*. The optical and metaphysical complexities of the situations in this picture demonstrate that it is as much about the artists' (sic) reflections on art and on the nature of image-making as it is a visual memento of the appearance of family members.

A parallel set of complex functions involving several different sorts of images and images of other works of art again finds a principal locus in Manet, in his *Portrait of Emile Zola* (1868), where the accoutrements of the sitter have many revealing functions in regard to him (and the artist) that go beyond conventional symbolic references. Again, Ensor, and more recently, Barnes, Neel, and Sleigh have exploited these kinds of possibilities in their works, and Abrons appears to welcome these connections. Her painting *Robert Lucy in My Studio* (1995, cat. no. 8) not only documents the connection between the two artists as sitter and model, but also clearly recalls, especially in the relaxed and lolling pose of the sitter and his bold facial expression, the later works of Neel, portraits of younger artists and writers in her circle.

The metaphysical extension of meanings within a basic pictorial category is addressed differently in Jackson's work, where the nude, portrait, self-portrait, and metaphysical subject are often mixed, as with the other artists discussed here. But Jackson retains clear references to another kind of image in his work—the photograph. The photographs (and, perhaps even more germanely, printed reproductions of them) that interest him are of specific types: he has formed a large collection of magazines and scrapbooks of various images, mostly of "beefcake" magazines, sensational crime and gossip tabloids, and anthologies of male nudes, frequently with a strong (homo)erotic flavor. Being informed by such a quantity of this material, Jackson's most straightforward images of either himself or the model are pervaded with the sense of the *louche*, the somewhat disreputable and anti-social. Whatever the expressions of his figures, and they are frequently unusual, the effect of Jackson's paintings is very much "in your face," with a powerful whiff of the potential violence of much street and pop-music culture.

Jackson combines this modern reference, however, with an awareness of the history of grand-manner painting; and so in his untitled reclining male nude of 1993 (cat. no. 20), we see that he has given his saucily confrontational figure the air of Goya's *Nude Maja* (c. 1795-1805) and has connected it with the Venetian tradition of the reclining Venus that is also

behind Manet's *Olympia*. In this way, Jackson brings off something analogous to but quite different from Sleigh's achievement in her well-known gender-reversal images of male nudes posed as odalisques, *majas*, and Venuses. Neither Jackson nor Sleigh is being satirical here in the sense of presenting us with a visual gag (although the paintings are undeniably witty and fun); rather, each artist addresses the deeper issue of why such a pose, if compositionally, artistically, and expressively suitable for one sex, should not work just as well for the other. We know about the importance of this question from the earlier work of Margaret Mead in her anthropological studies of the social and gender roles of several Oceanic peoples. The association of gender reversal with shamanistic roles in a number of cultures is also apposite to the images of Jackson and Sleigh. Each is concerned with what is beyond expected norms and boundaries and how such "exceptions" (if that is what they are) are related to forms, images, and meanings regarded as mainstream to this or that culture, especially *ours*.

Positioning his figures on the canvas, Jackson employs an intimidating closeness which makes them seem very near to us, a little nearer than is customary or comfortable. We feel a bit forced into an intimacy that is somewhat threatening. Jackson's occasional over-life-size scale contributes to this sense of uneasy proximity as well and recalls similar effects in the works of both Golub and Paschke. The profaneness of Jackson's monumental images causes us to relate them to troubling aspects of contemporary society at the same time that we must acknowledge them as extensions and acknowledgments of the Grand Manner of Western painting. His sometimes harsh tonal contrasts and deliberately limited palette connect the worlds of "high" and "low" images in another way, through their recollection of the intensified contrasts and expressive chromatism of magazine illustrations, even photomechanical ones.

The metaphysical current in each of our artists is most consistently presented in Gustin's grandiose compositions. The world of Gustin's vision is obviously "impossible" in the sense of our being able to imagine the situations he offers as occurring in the ordinary course of things. However, they press up to or just past the edge of what might be possible in an elaborate stage or studio set-up. In this way, we are taken far from the realm of the everyday and into the areas of dream, compound memory, imagination, and art. Gustin's inventions and visual constructs are given to us with a degree and kind of realization which allows us to accept them as "observed" by the artist and the viewer. His figures speak of a deep knowledge of the human form and its varieties gained from long observation and study of the body itself and of other works of art. There is a deliberate display of virtuosity in their poses and the angles from which we view them: very often the model could not possibly have held the pose for more than a few seconds, and the ability to present such figures, so striking in attitude and so credible to our familiar visual systems, is both magical and delightful.

The scale of Gustin's paintings and of the forms and images in them places his efforts in comparison to monumental fresco painting; the energetic compositional movements and the shifting and strong color are scenographic in an operatic way. This expansiveness of vision is exhilarating in itself, and Gustin's manneristic, compressed and exploding spatial effects can make them dynamically thrilling. In all these regards, his primacy of visual invention and rich baroque fantasy in every composition set him a bit apart from the other five artists here, but each of them does suggest, in addition to their numerous other involvements, an unbroken connection with metaphysical visionary experience. Their works always display some strong degree of poetic meaning, numinous awareness, or oneiric dimensions. Gustin is almost always in this territory, and with the other artists this sort of experience is always present, even in "ordinary" visions.

There are clear connections in Gustin's work with Mannerism—Giulio Romano's frescoes in the Palazzo del Té and Pellegrino Tibaldi's Genoese ceilings, for instance—and with the baroque style of Rubens, as well as with their continuation in the nineteenth century in Delacroix and Géricault. Gustin has links in this century with Spencer's eccentric visions, mentioned above with regard to advanced notions of the nude and nude self-portrait, and with Edwin Dickinson and Ben Kamihira. Associations with Leslie are also apparent, especially with his series of mural-scale pictures about the death of Frank O'Hara (1967-75), and also with two important figures closely anticipating some of

Gustin's concerns, McGarrell and Barnes. Both of them (unlike Leslie) operate exclusively in the mythic world of metaphysical visions and have done so consistently since the mid-1950s. Both have approached the mural scale in monumental compositions and explore a very complex, layered set of imagistic references, literary allusions, private symbolism, and penetrating psychological awareness. If anything, Barnes's and McGarrell's works are even denser and more replete with optical incident than Gustin's, and the hermeticism of their meaning and content demands an interpretive approach of considerable sophistication. Gustin's content is perhaps a bit more accessible.

To some degree, passages of pure painting are subsumed in the convincing presentation of his strange and provocative images. However, the intricacy of Gustin's painting invites close inspection, and his surfaces often have a dull sheen like that of leather or the waxy patina of old frescoes. This sense of the *matière* is interesting in itself and recalls similar features in the work of such artists as Balthus and Lennart Anderson, whose surfaces are often a kind of tinted crust, not entirely smooth but dully pitted like the skin of an orange. Gustin's wipings and traces of the brush leave no doubt about the significance of process and gesture to the artist, but it is the muscular dynamism of his compositions and operatic grandeur of the subjects that dominate. This is essential in such large paintings lest the totality of the active vision be compromised and become insufficiently coherent to be fully grasped.

The special tartness of Gustin's color distinguishes him as an accomplished and idiosyncratic master of it; his taste, at present at any rate, runs to the high-key and acid set off with very telling contrasts of darker hues and values. Gustin's color has an unusual atmospheric aspect: intricate images of shadows, clouds, reflected lights, and modulations of color under lighting conditions of varying intensity allow the artist a great play with related hues in differing tones. His manipulations of blues and hot oranges and reds can set up shimmering chromatic shifts over what we read as the surface of a single discrete part of the image. Working together with broken, intersecting, and overlapping forms and spatial structures, this color virtuosity is a major focus of Gustin's compositional attentions, and he is able to direct it to emphasize the metaphysical sense generated by the entire image.

In fact, all six of the artists here display an exceptionally elaborate command of color, though this is less obvious in the recent works of Jackson, who currently opts for wringing chromatic richness out of a limited palette. In this way, Jackson's evolution is the reverse of Pearlstein's: Jackson's earlier color was very high-key (and may be again). Each artist utilizes his or her color constructs in several ways at once: the color has a good deal to do with emotional tone and metaphysical aspect, it usually operates as a compositional structure in and of itself, and it manages our ways of understanding the whole image by helping define aspects of the imagery. In this last consideration, the defining color is not necessarily local, that is, the color of the object seen by the artist. Often the color is invented even if the form is observed or remembered, and this autonomous kind of color is an important element distinguishing our artists from those interested in "optical fidelity."

One of the principal points the present exhibition attempts to establish is that a major aspect of modernist sensibility, in fact much of what we characterize as the development of modern art, is a living continuation of the great current in Western painting since the Renaissance that is known as the Grand Manner. The nexus of this tradition and one of the crucial origins of modernism occurs in Manet's paintings of the early 1860s as well as in Courbet and even early Degas. In the view of many, modernism should be seen as arising with the reactive directions of Romanticism; from this perspective, the links are Géricault and Delacroix. Still earlier conjunctions of modernist concerns and traditional forms and ideas have been traced well into the middle of the eighteenth century by Robert Rosenblum and others engaged in uncovering the roots of Romanticism and its relationship to Neo-classicism. Various facets of what may be considered the classical (or Neo-classical) esthetic are themselves an element of modernism; such connections can be found not only in the obvious example of Picasso but more unexpectedly in Duchamp by 1921. This would be a challenging theme for another exhibition exploring features of current modernism, one which might extend beyond the category of figure painting. However, the nature of our perceptual processes and the methods by which we interpret them—how we find meaning in our experience—situates figurative art at the core of modernist esthetics.

EPILOGUE

The accomplishments of our six artists, or at least the works shown here, do not constitute a visual manifesto to any extent greater than that created by a single work of art. While the artists are all aware of one another's work, and several are acquainted, their association resides in shared concerns about the potential and nature of painting, especially its metaphysical qualities and those features which simultaneously illuminate aspects of art and of all experience. A number of interesting professional links among these artists may or may not account for such common interests. Doud, Gustin, and Willenbrink are currently on the faculty of the painting department of The School of the Art Institute of Chicago; Doud, Jackson, and Lucy are alumni of the SAIC, and Lucy studied at Northwestern with Paschke, also an SAIC alumnus. Abrons' husband, David Sharpe, whose example she says was critical in reaching her definition and maturity as a painter, is also an SAIC graduate. While the artists in this exhibition were not chosen because of these perhaps fortuitous connections, such links indicate many important yet little-known effects of the SAIC studio and, the alumni here say, art history programs. This is significant evidence that modern art now is still very much a pluralistic heterogeneity consisting of many diverse and even opposing tendencies and directions. ❧

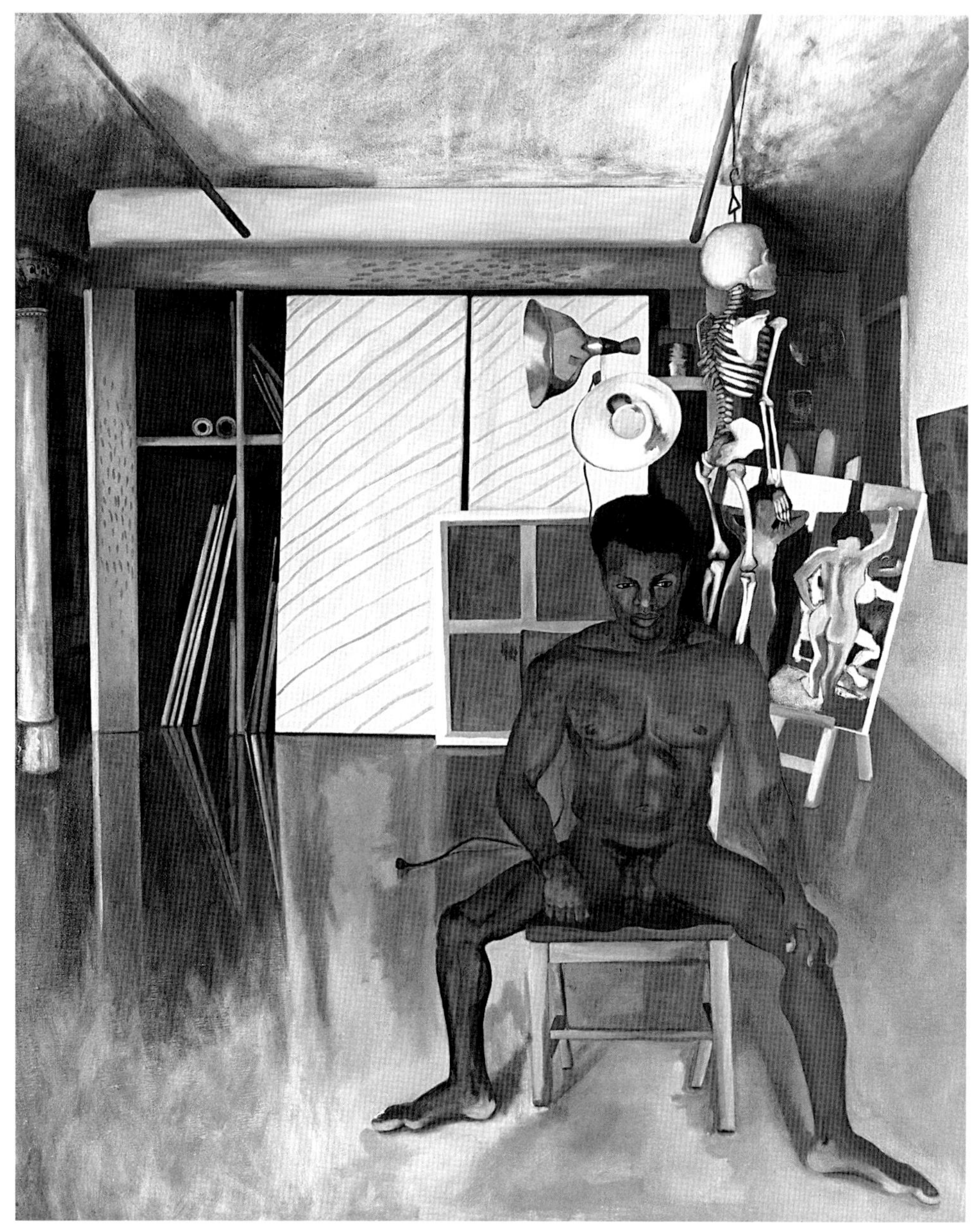

Seated Model in the Studio, 1993

COLOR PLATES

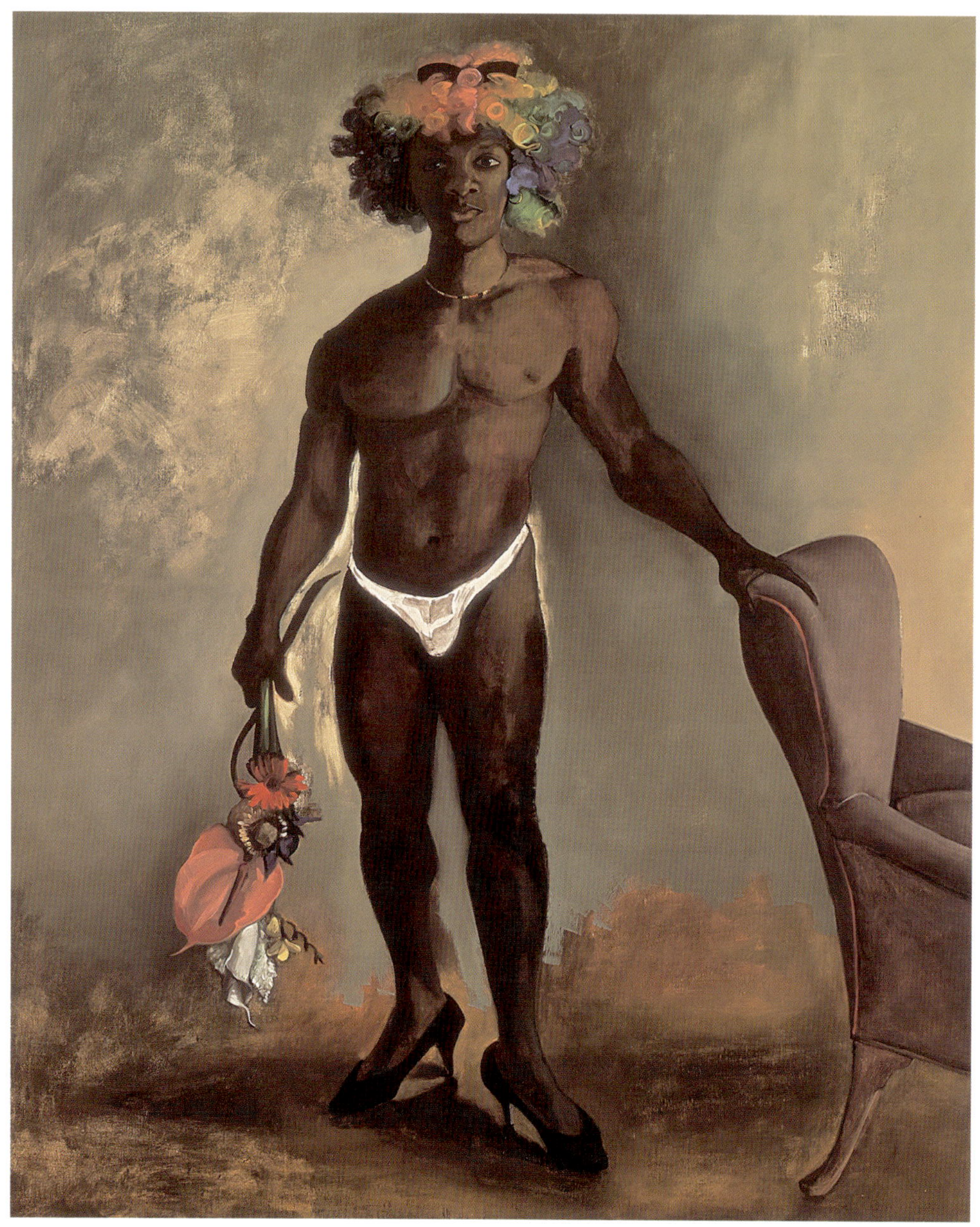

Ken in Gay Pride Parade Costume, 1994

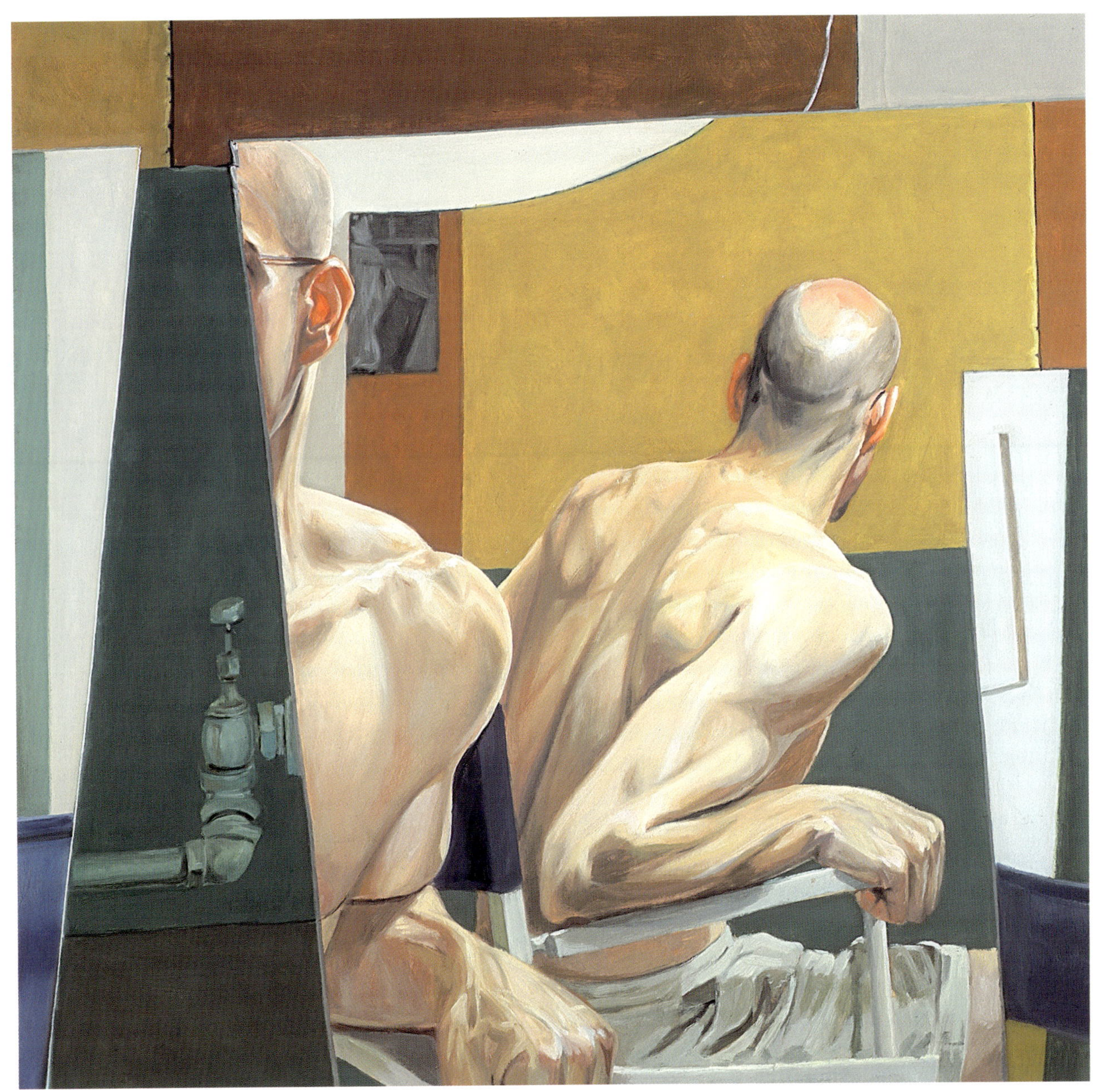

Francisco St. (CK), 1995

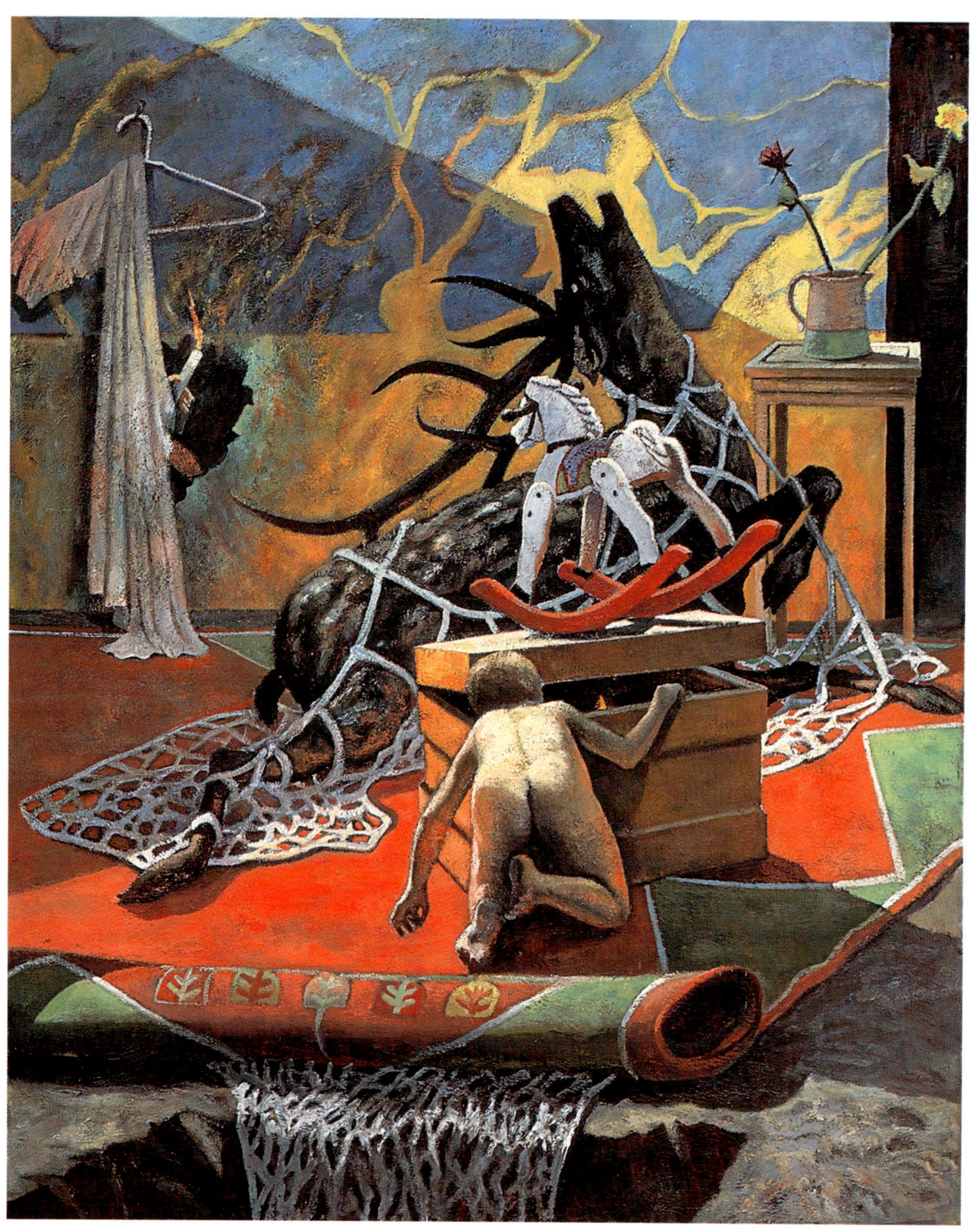

First Scene, 1993-95

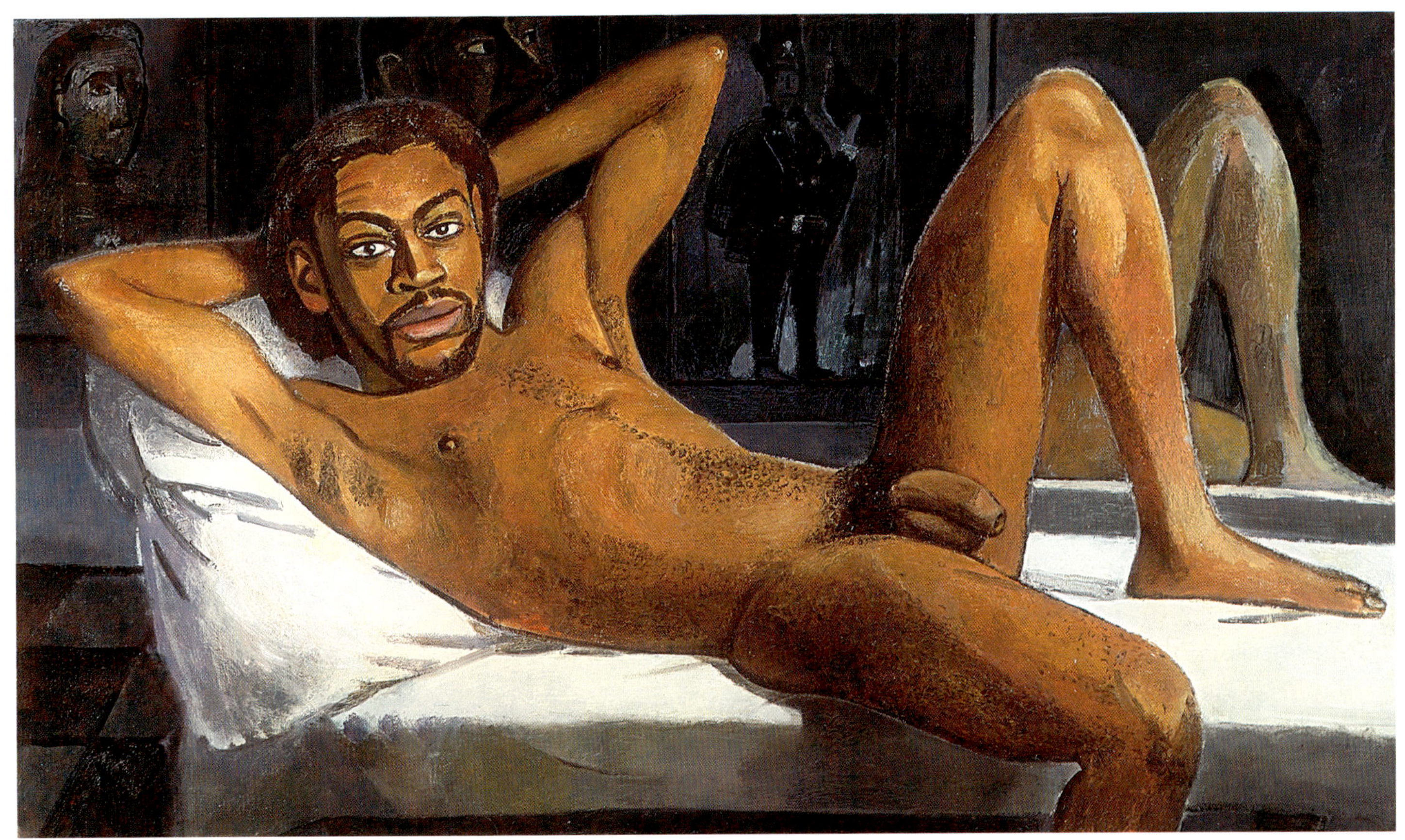

Untitled, 1993

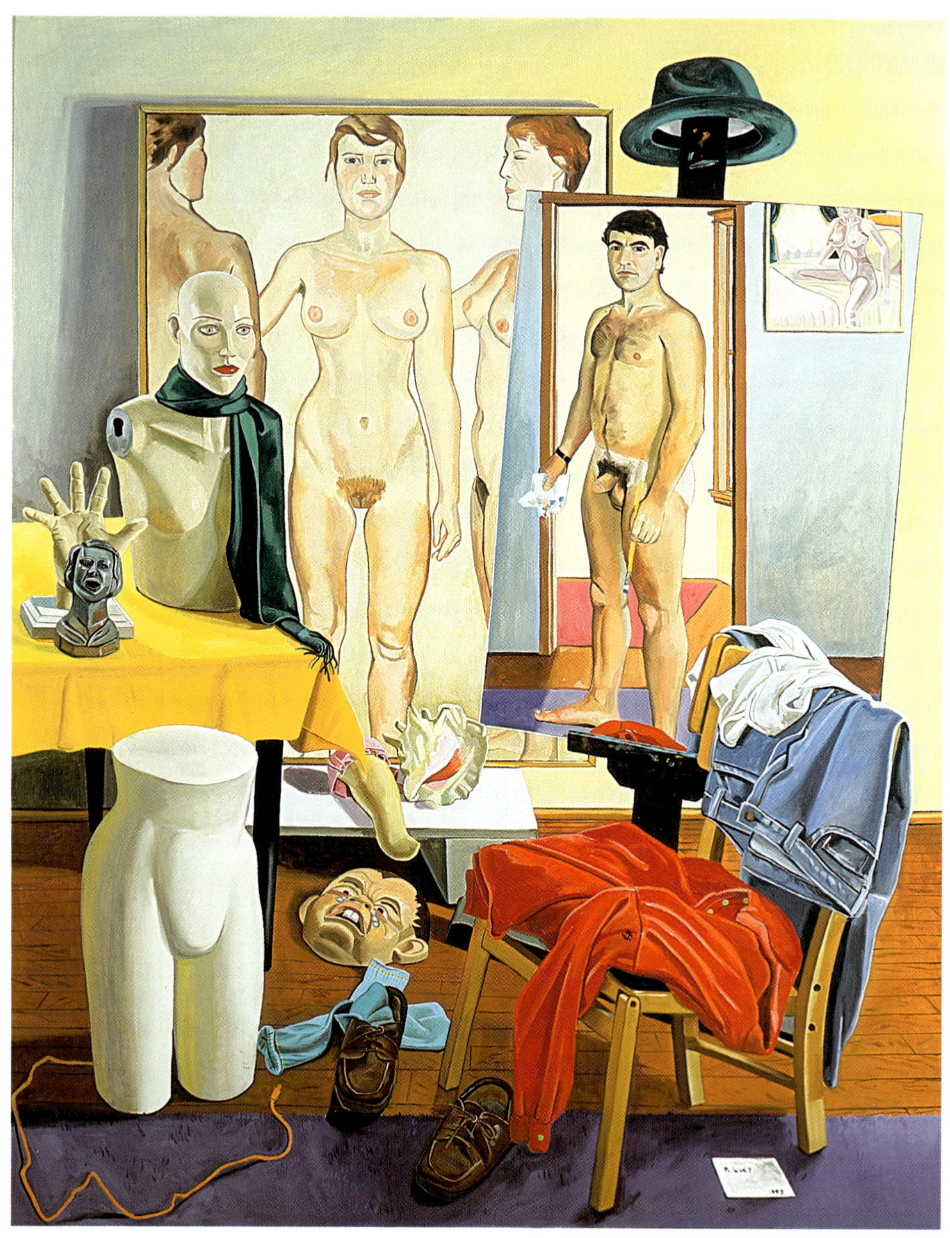

Artist and Models, 1993

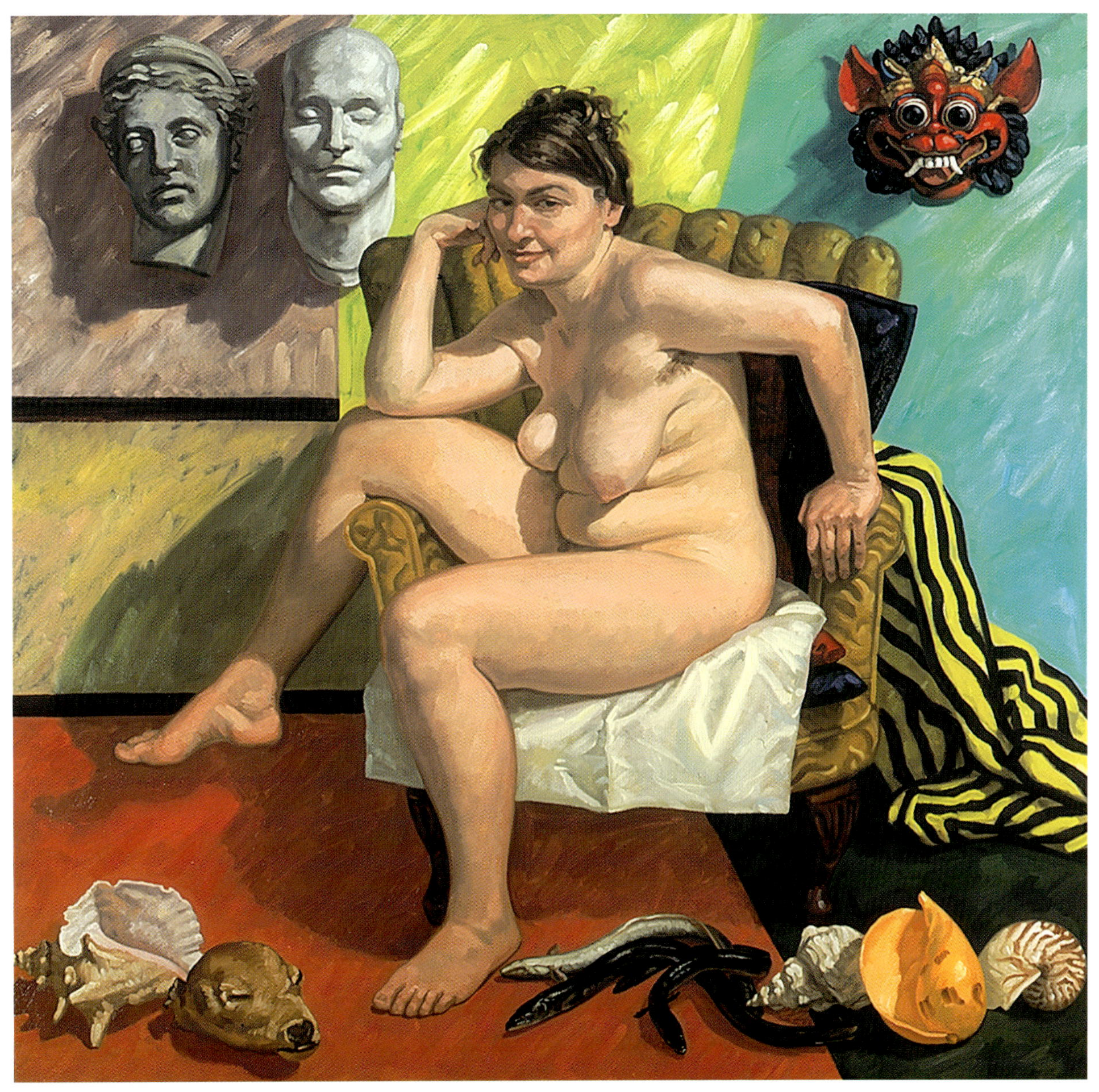

Seated Model in the Studio, 1995

ANNE *abrons*

The subjects of Anne Abrons' figure paintings are connected directly with her daily life; they frequently show the artist herself, her children, her husband (also a painter), models, and friends in her artistic milieu. Within this scope, which necessarily includes a good deal of emphasis on the domestic, Abrons takes on allegorical themes, psychological probings of identity and representations of it, societal tropes of one sort or another, keen examinations of the nature of perception, and a range of grand-manner painting types and formats from different periods. Abrons' work is deeply thoughtful, but it is not the result of contrived conceptualizing about what all ought to go in it. She inhabits a world of sensibility in which her artistic issues *are* the day-to-day issues (along with more familiar ones), and she is unyielding in her pursuit of the most effective involvements with them. Despite its seriousness, Abrons' work has an engaging freshness of vision and unpretentious candor: her seriousness is so matter-of-fact that it is not intimidating but instead invites us to find out what she has to show us—on many different levels.

Much of the intricacy of these paintings comes from their spatial structures, often complicated with tipped planes, dramatic foreshortenings, compressions, and dynamic vectors. Abrons' manipulation of these elements provides a restless sense of movement, even when her subjects seem static. This liveliness is also carried out in her brushwork, which is vigorous and decisive, forming pulsing shoals of strokes of different orientations throughout each composition. While Abrons' subjects belong to familiar categories of painting—the model seated in the studio, standing nude, group family portrait, and the portrait, full- or half-length, standing or seated—she brings to these themes significant other dimensions which are part of her own viewpoint. In *Seated Model in the Studio* (1993, cat. no. 5), the studio space with its vast, clear floor and distant closet racks for paintings makes up a meaningful reflection on the model's situation. He is swamped in the space, vulnerable in his nudity, noble in his patience and exposed humanness (of which nudity is such an important image), and has a curious role as a possible participant in the creation of paintings which we see either stacked in the racks or turned

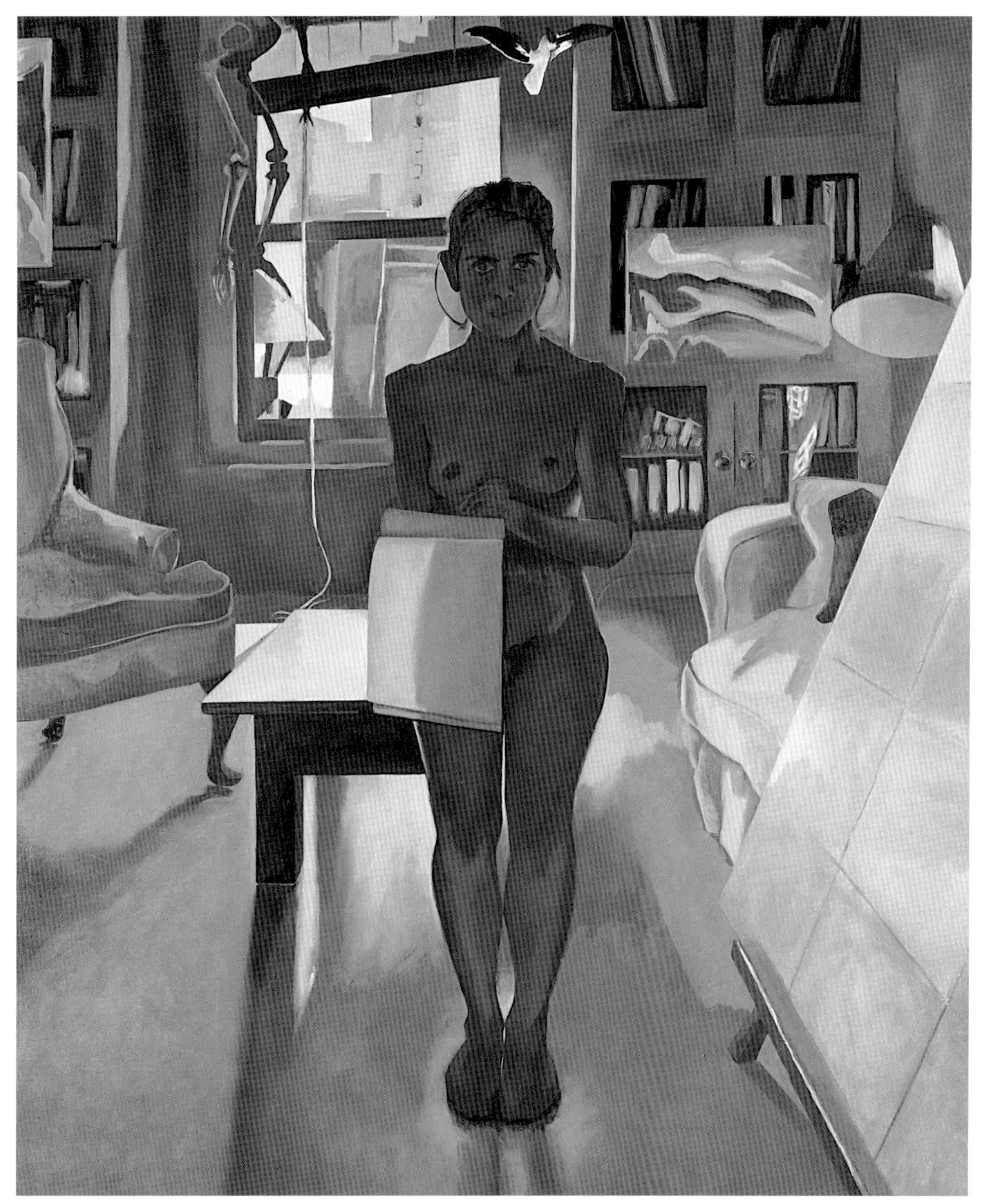

Nude Self-Portrait, 1995

CATALOGUE № 7

away from us at the back of the room.

The image of the painting in the painting, a metaphysical theme since antiquity, is one that Abrons employs with unusual skill. Sometimes these images are of her own work, raising a mystifying question: in just what sense is the "Abrons in the Abrons" a painting *by* Abrons? When the work depicted is identifiably by another artist, issues of homage or other attitudes towards this work of art and its author also come into play. Images of mirror reflections introduce additional considerations, such as philosophical as well as optical reflection. The image of the painting turned away from the viewer, as in the seated-model picture just described, recurs in *Annette Maryan in My Studio* (1990, cat. no. 1), where Abrons sets a wall of such pictures behind the sitter. The edges of the canvases, the sections wrapped around the stretchers, the stretcher bars, and their braces all form a strongly architectonic progression of foreshortened rectangles. As these forms decrease in size toward the background and are set at an angle to the picture plane, they create a vertiginous recession which the sitter, twisting in her chair, stabilizes through the sheer force of character expressed in her striking features. The intersecting braces of the large stretched canvas seen directly behind the figure of Mme. Maryan pin her just at the geographic center of the composition. The stretcher bars make up a kind of squarish halo or aureole—the shape used in Byzantine and some *trecento* Italian art to indicate the spiritual eminence of a living

person (as opposed to the round halo of a saint).

Abrons' portrait of her husband, *David: Night Portrait* (1992, cat. no. 2), takes on a compositional idea also dealt with by Impressionists such as Degas and Sisley. Here the half-length figure is off to one side, with still-life elements and indications of setting dominating much of the canvas. In many pictures of this type, the sitter is shown as either unaware of the viewer or artist (Abrons' sitter is asleep) or inattentive to them, looking away and to the side. The candid view and figure-cropping very likely have some connection with precedents in informal photography and similar effects in Japanese woodcuts. At any rate, pushing the image of the sitter away from the center—the ordinary place of honor—paradoxically both calls attention to it and relegates or at least demotes it to a level of importance shared by the still life. This is a way of alluding to a complex interplay of nature, human existence, compositional arrangements of things, and to mortality (one of the still-life objects is a skull "regarding" the sleeping sitter). All these elements, together with Abrons' rich color and luxuriant paint handling, make this work an unusual, intensely focused artistic achievement. —*D.A.*

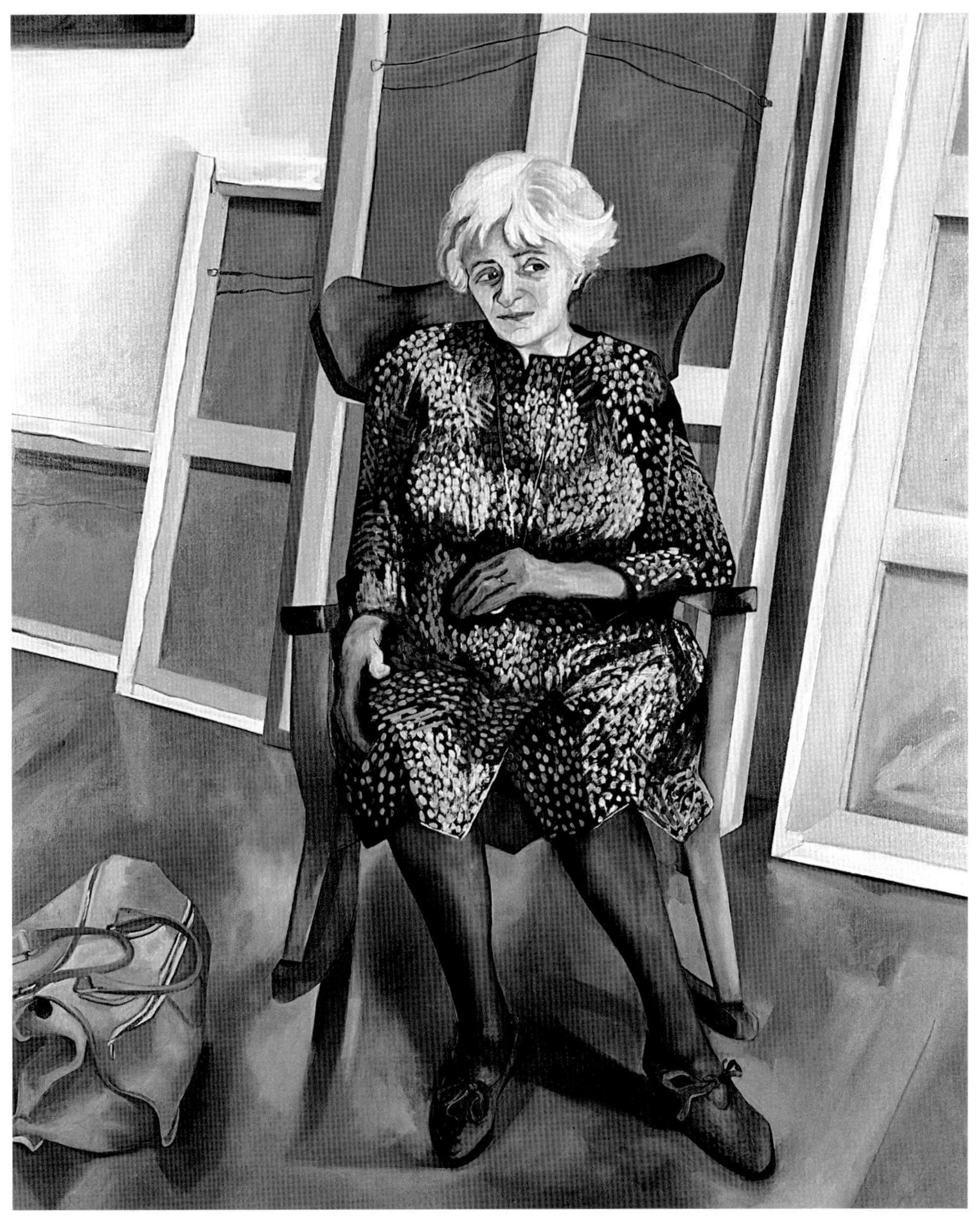

Annette Maryan in My Studio, 1990

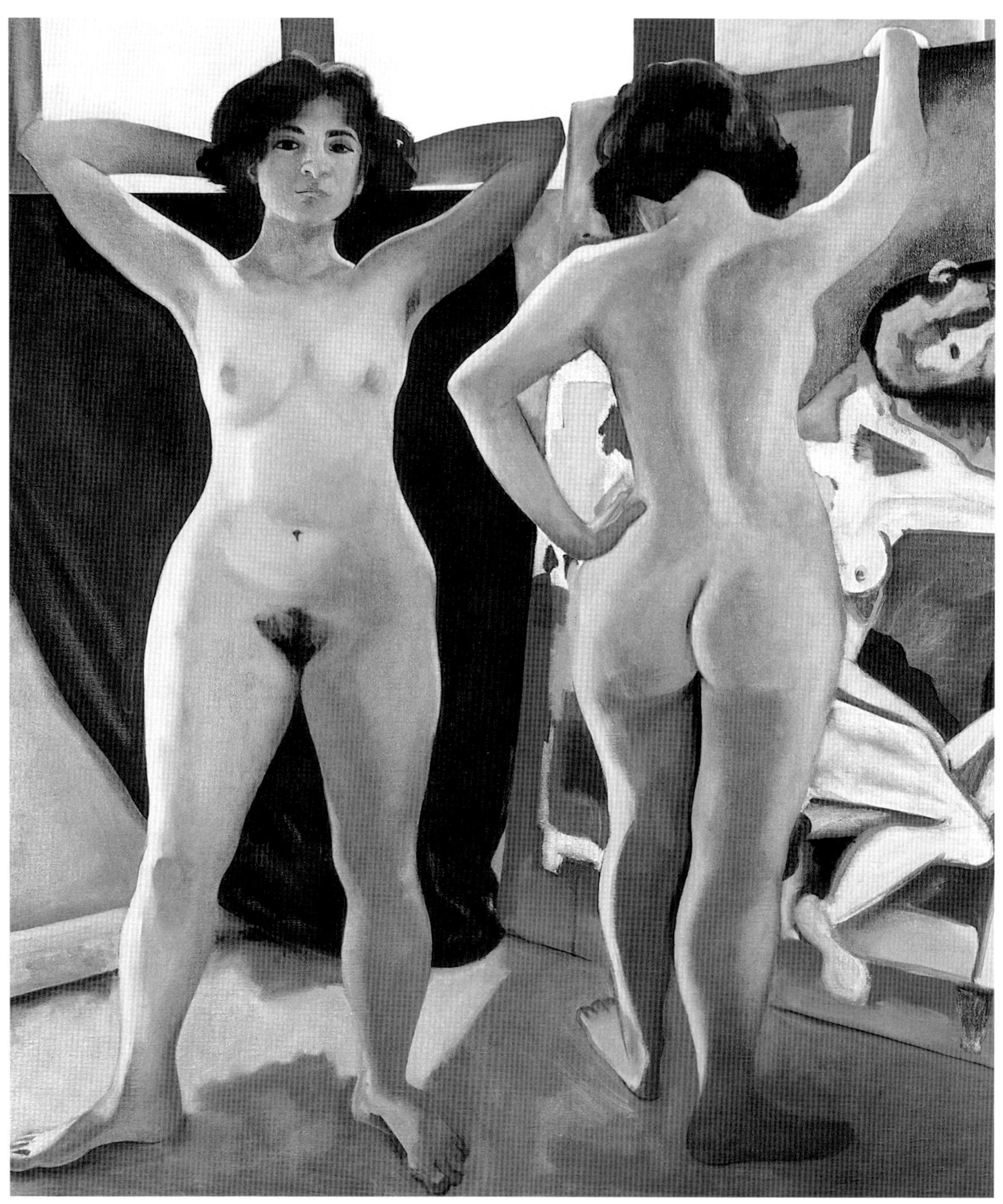

Double Ondine, 1992

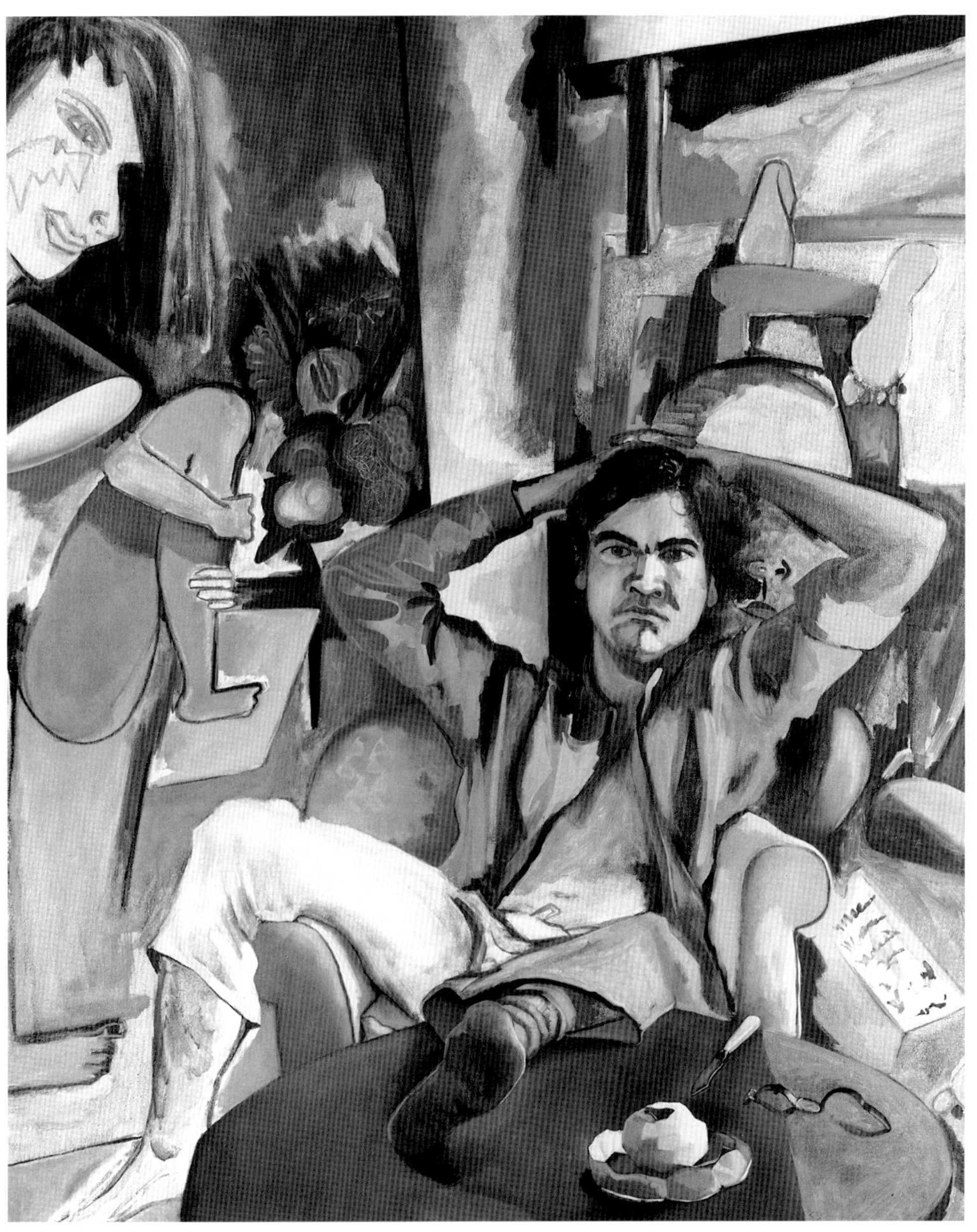

Robert Lucy in My Studio, 1995

CATALOGUE № 8

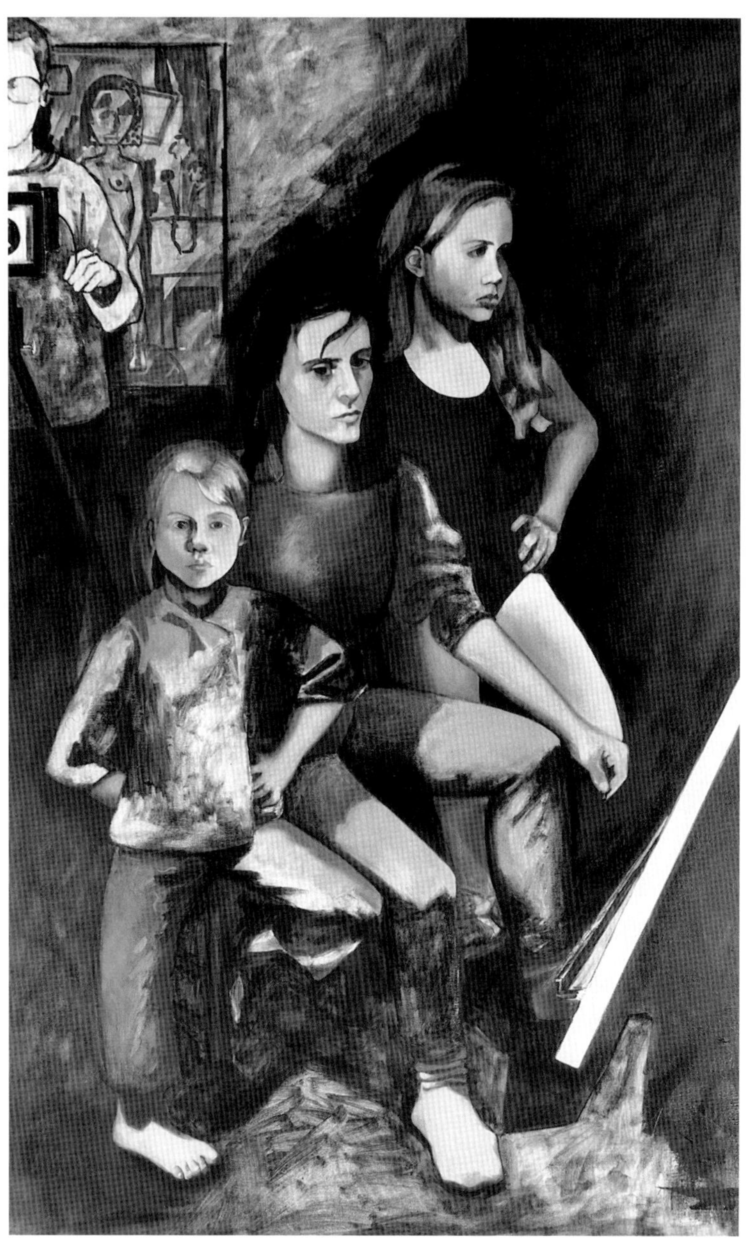

Family Portrait, 1993

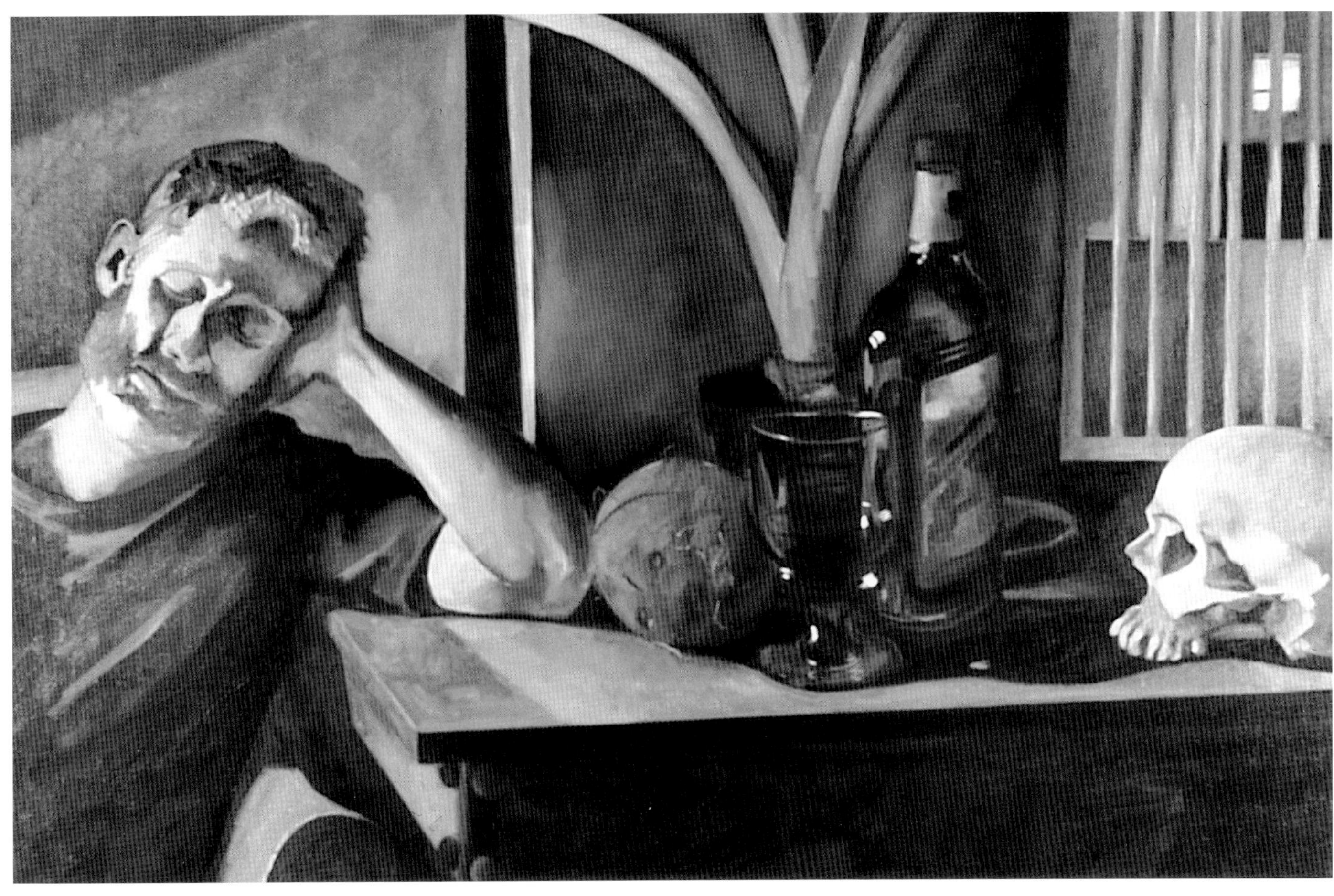

David: Night Portrait, 1992

CATALOGUE № 2

TIM *d o u d*

Tim Doud's rigorous concentration on major issues of figure painting, the nude and the portrait, has lately resulted in an increasing monumentality and emphatic figural presence in each painting. Some of this seems due to his employment of a life-size scale (or one close to it); at times in his previous work he dealt with smaller formats wherein the force of his painterly realization was belied or somewhat diminished—the figures sometimes seemed a bit too small to precipitate the fullest degree of connection between them and the viewer. These smaller scale (and size) works are not lesser achievements than any of his others, but they do accept the limitations of such an intimate format and the small nudes, especially, cry to be given a more ample scale. For the past several years, a larger scale has brought Doud to greater command over the complex forms of his figures, and has also allowed his lively brushwork fuller play.

Interestingly, Doud preserves in these larger works some of the intimacy of feeling that distinguished the earlier ones, establishing an emotive tone about the nudes which is distinctively his own. Often framing his figures (or the sections we see of them) with detailed elements of furniture, Doud sets up a low viewpoint that takes us very near his model and suggests a kind of familiarity with the figure *as a person*. Because these nudes do not seem to react to us, we are able to examine them at our leisure; in so doing, we can allow the emotional affects of the visual situation to develop fully, appreciate the structural clarity and intricacy with which the artist has presented the figure, and take in the careful effects of color, brushwork, and tonal composition central to Doud's artistic concerns.

Doud's portraits (including self-portraits) offer experiences in some ways emotionally parallel to those of his nudes, but the artist is also at pains to make clear the unique aspects of his sitters' identities. *Bishop Frank Griswold* (1994-95, cat. no. 11) gives us a warm and penetrating sense of the bishop's personality, with his clerical function indicated by his robes, crozier, the picture on the wall behind him, and so forth. Doud's way of showing the bishop allows us to imagine a relationship with the

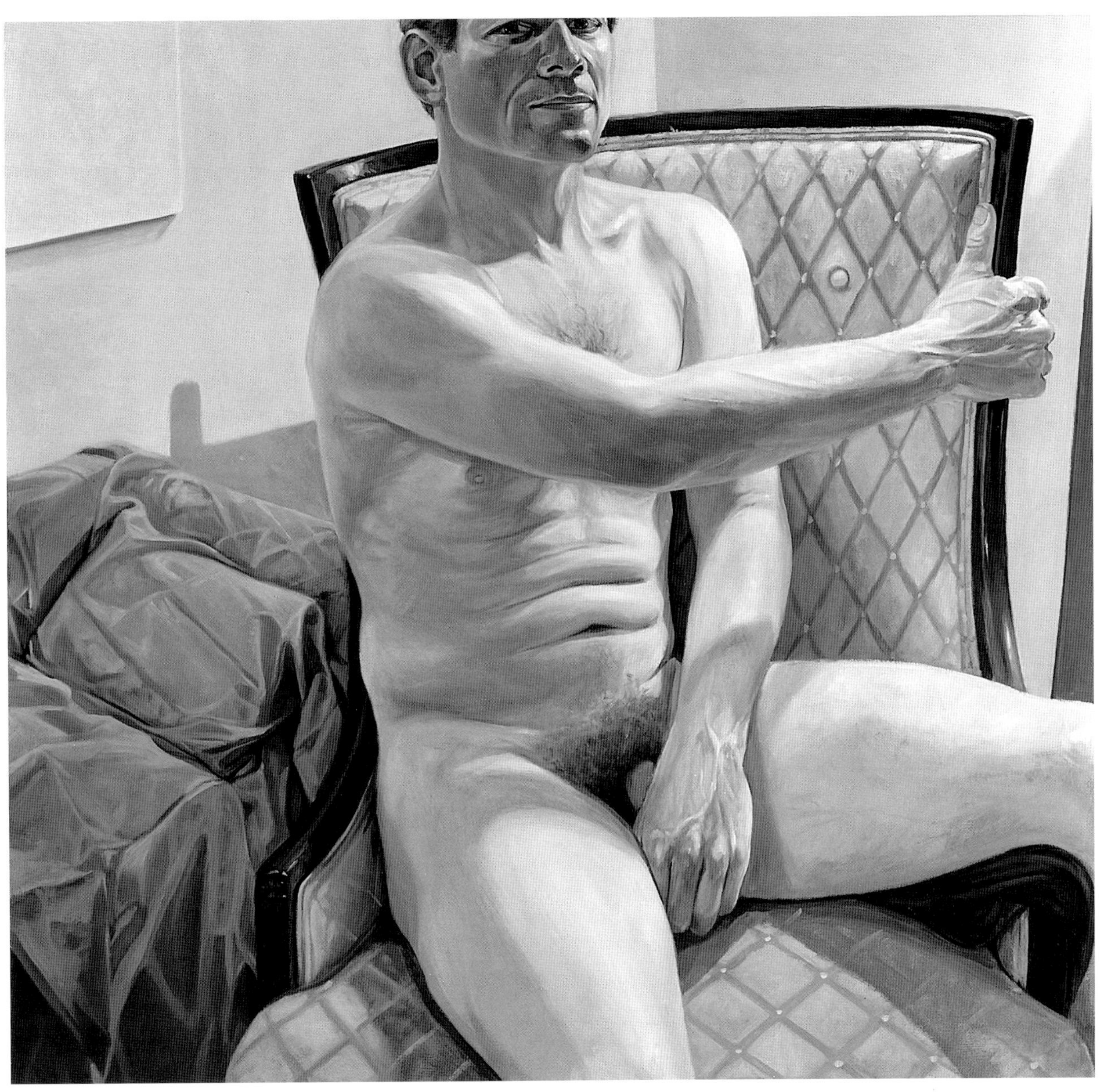

Halstead (Portrait II), 1994-95

CATALOGUE № 12

personality the artist has discovered and revealed. In other portraits, particularly some interesting group ones, Doud invites us to engage in an interpretive process of "psyching out" the sitters, their relationships to one another and to the artist. This process can only attain esthetic significance if the visual structure in all its aspects, the composition in every sense of the word, has an integrity of design and order which can be appreciated for itself while we are in the act of "reading" the sitters.

Doud's self-portraits generate an electric concentration of mood, which presumably results from his fulfilling the double and simultaneous functions of sitter and artist. The additional dimensions here are those of the nude self-portrait, the artist's exploration and presentation of his attitudes and ideas about himself, both as a physical being and an artist. The sense of self-awareness in these pictures is often pervaded by a kind of discomfort and even anguish—perhaps about the very intensity of his own sensibilities. This is an existential facet of Doud's work, which unites the tradition of his direction—figure painting—with a contemporary spirit of uncertainty, harshness, and unease. A peculiar condition of this blend of feeling and intricacy of pictorial conception is that the unsettling emotional climate does not cancel out a sense of joy and satisfaction in painting. This quality appears as well in the other five artists in the exhibition. His exultation in the processes of painting allied with the communication of complex awareness gives Doud's oeuvre its durably gratifying character as much as the truth of what he may have to say in any given work.

It will be interesting to see if the increasing monumentality of Doud's undertakings leads him to explore compositions with several nudes or a group of figures other than the portrait. The general feeling of his work to date indicates that he has an emotional concern, a way of looking at the world of human relationships, and offers a compelling mix of intimacy and isolation that might be displayed still more fully in multifarious figure compositions. Such a direction, which may already be adumbrated in the complexity of Doud's nude self-portraits in this exhibition, would very likely involve more complicated spatial considerations than the other works in the present group demonstrate. In any event, Doud's accomplishments are very considerable, and not the least of them is his revelation of many further potentials. —*D.A.*

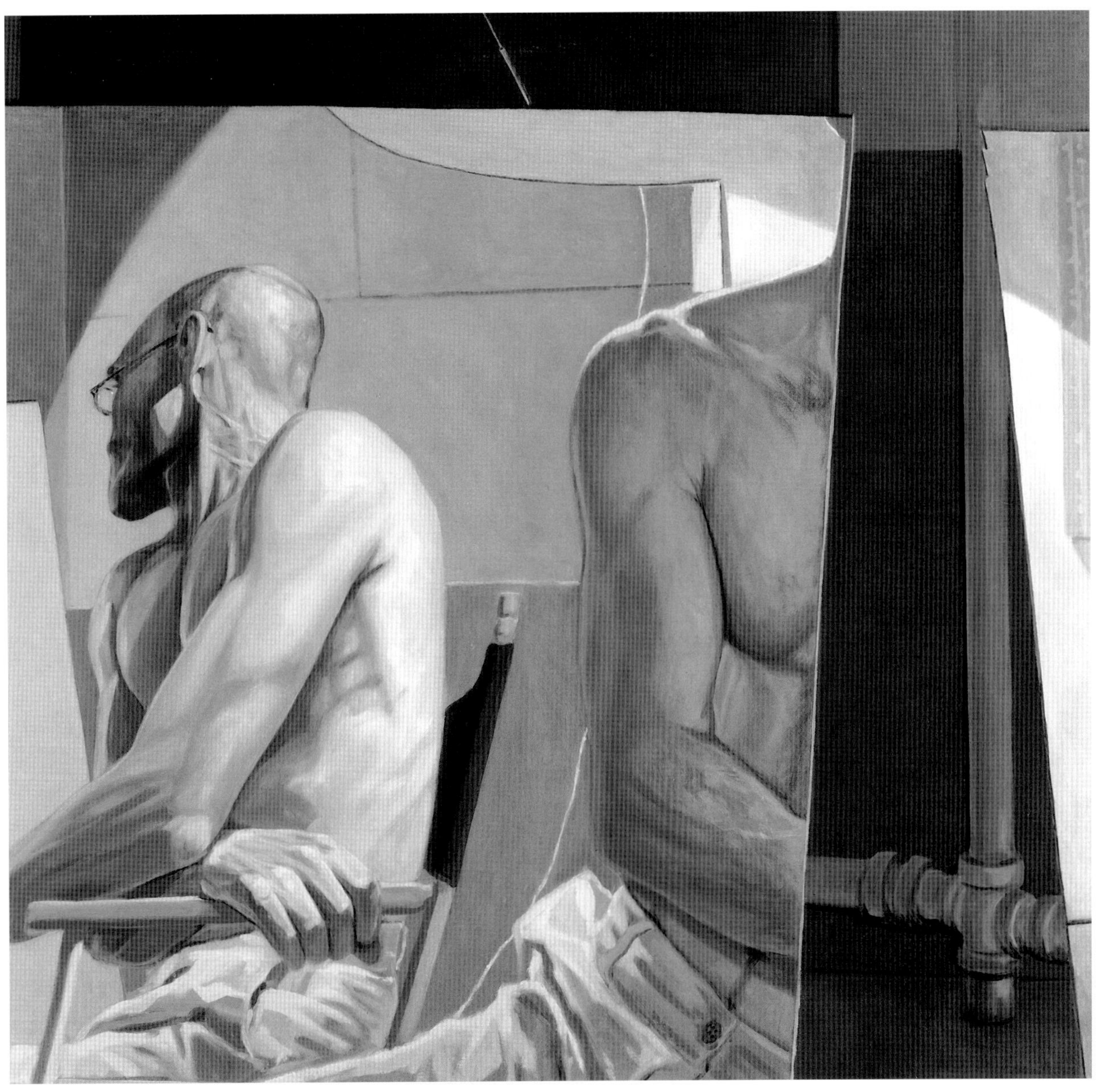

Francisco St. (CK II), 1995

CATALOGUE № 14

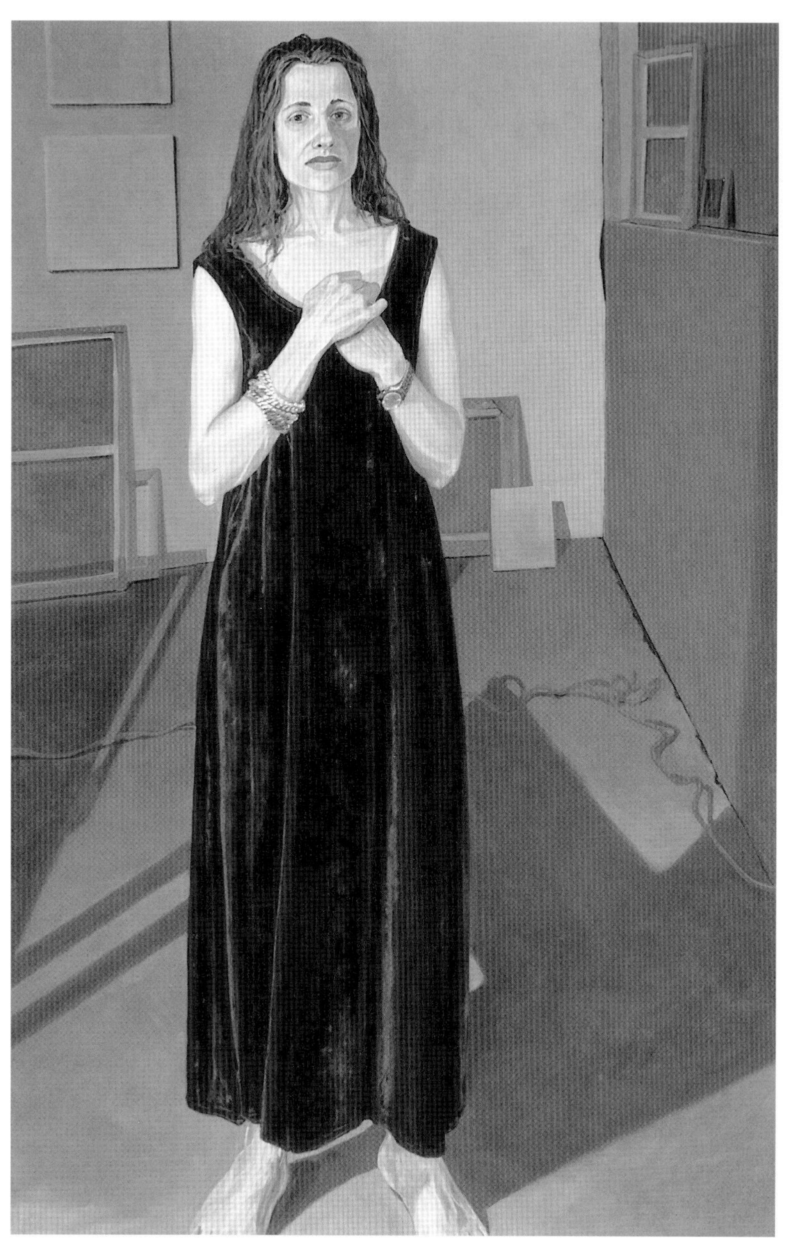

Giulietta, 1995

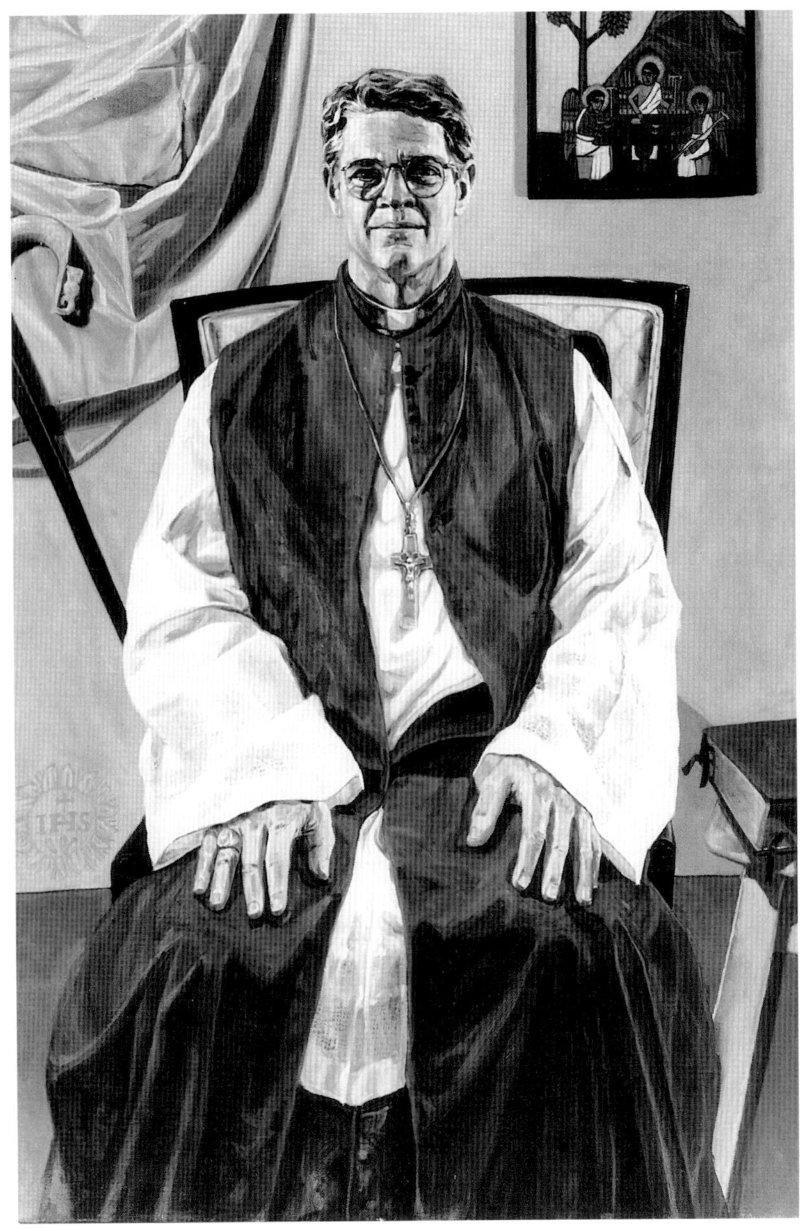

Bishop Frank Griswold, 1994-95

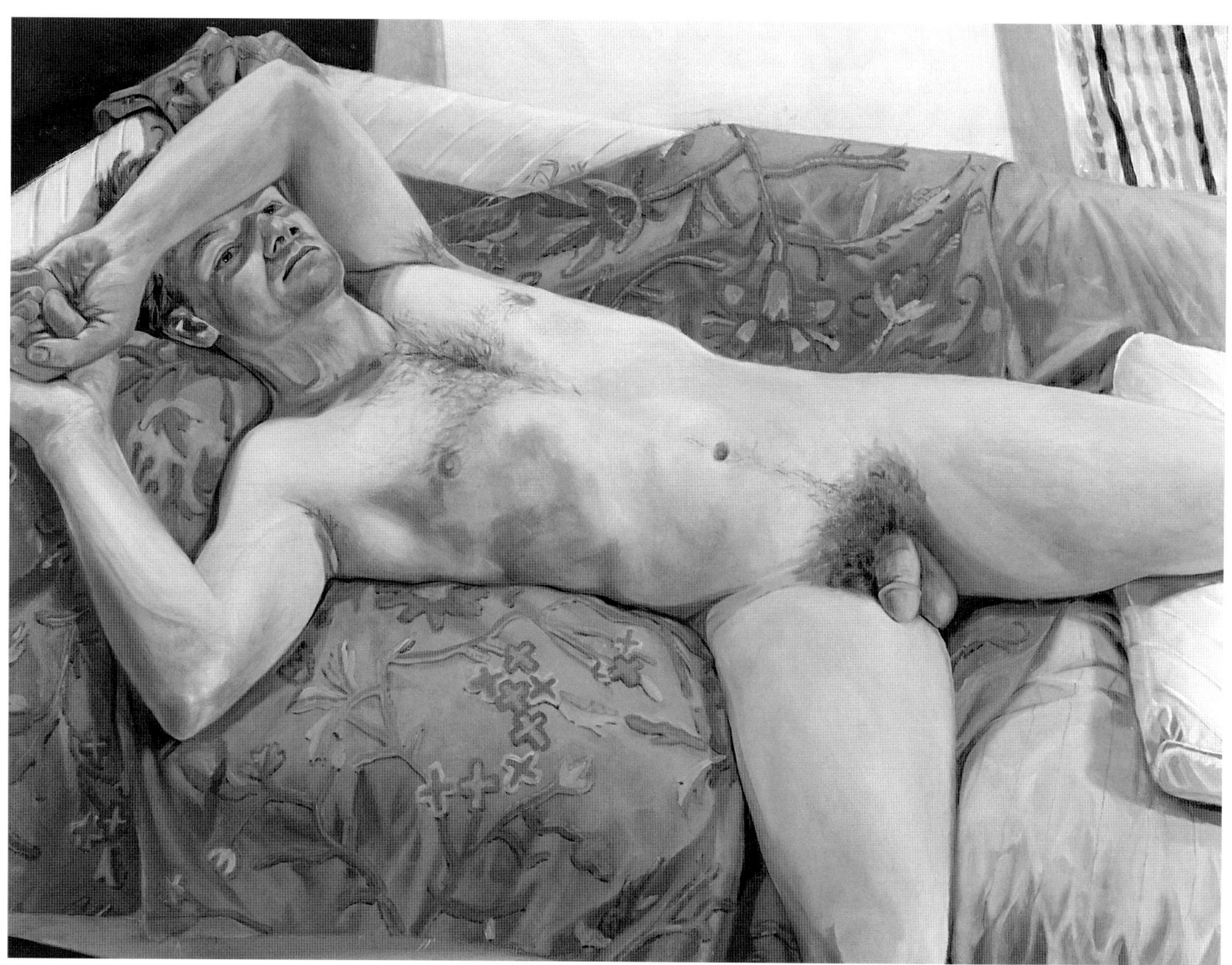

Halstead (Studio Blanket), 1994

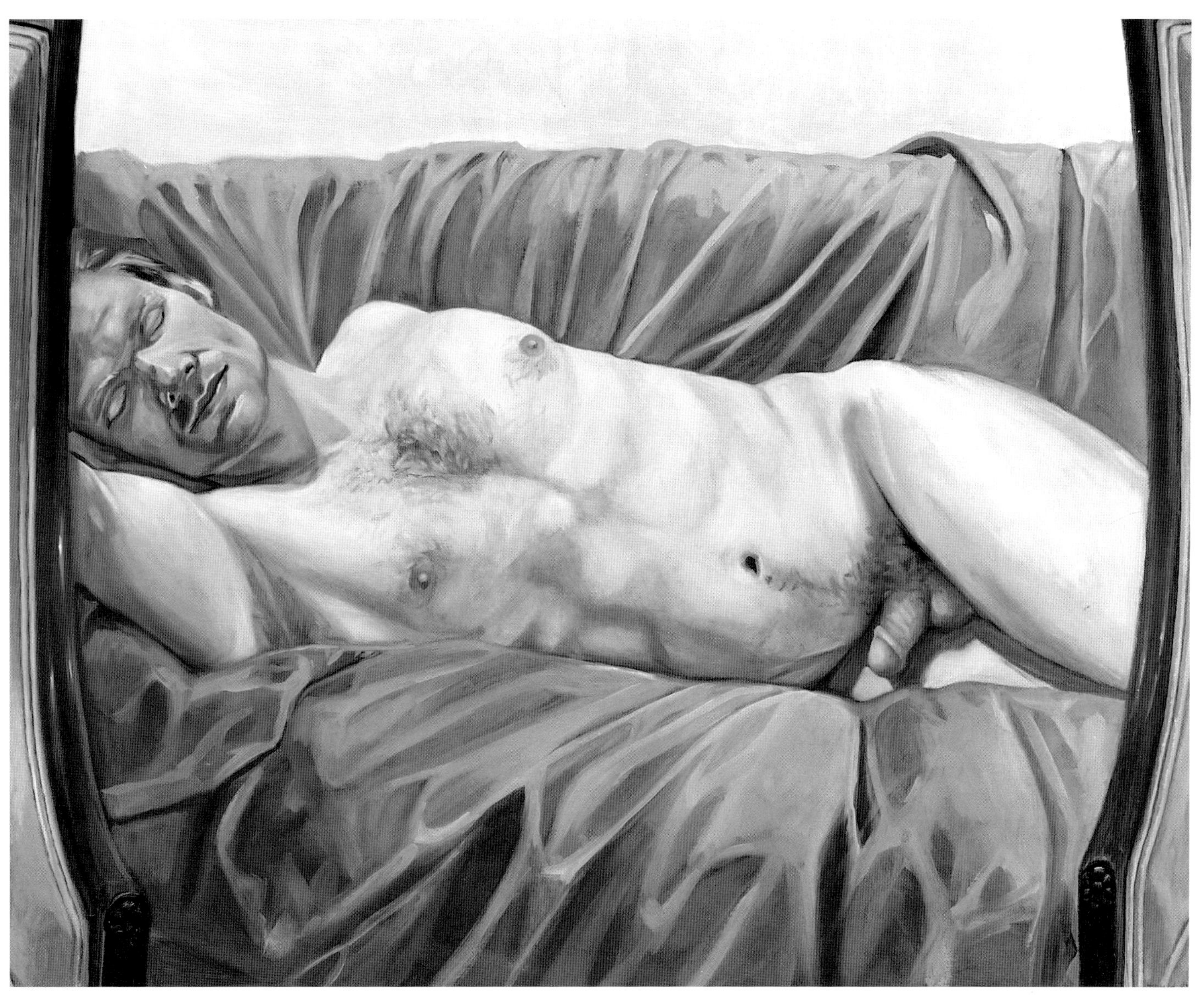

Halstead, 1993

DAN *gustin*

Although limitations of space and the immense scale of Dan Gustin's paintings allow only two of his canvases to be included here, each presents such a rich assemblage of pictorial event, imagistic invention, and intricate compositional development that we can experience whole universes of artistic accomplishment in them. Gustin offers dramatically theatrical tableaux in which the figures seem caught up in a ritual, performance, or discovery of the nature of the self and its relationships to images and forms in art and life. Each picture is, in one way, a room in the artist's interior domain, and each chamber is filled with objects that reflect on nature, art, and their involvements in human existence. In *Untitled* (1994-95, cat. no. 17), a figure we may understand as that of the artist himself gropes and gestures within a mysterious cloud which obscures his features; this perhaps is the obstacle of ordinary perception. The figure faces the urban world, visible through a large window. In the room behind him, a pair of monumental nudes, each encumbered with an image or mask of an animal form, strides frantically through a studiolike interior. We see the overturned figure of a lawn jockey, on a partition wall a painting showing children with a bow and arrow, and, between the nude figures and that of the artist, a geometric painting, its cloudy glazing shattered in shards over the floor.

The metaphysics here seems to involve ordinary vision, the inner realm of the artist's memories, preoccupations, and images relating to him, and the methods and varieties of art which process this material. We need not construct a story, but it is essential to grasp the implications of Gustin's subject matter: nature as feral and as prey, the nude as an image of human aware-ness, the danger of the magical dimensions of image-making (the lion-headed nude carries what appear to be venomous serpents), and the types of consciousness we employ in interpreting our experience and environment. These are large themes and demand the scale Gustin has given them. The sheer expanse of surface also allows him to arrogate the mural scale and to display his virtuosity in painting, pictorial invention, and rich color in a very full measure.

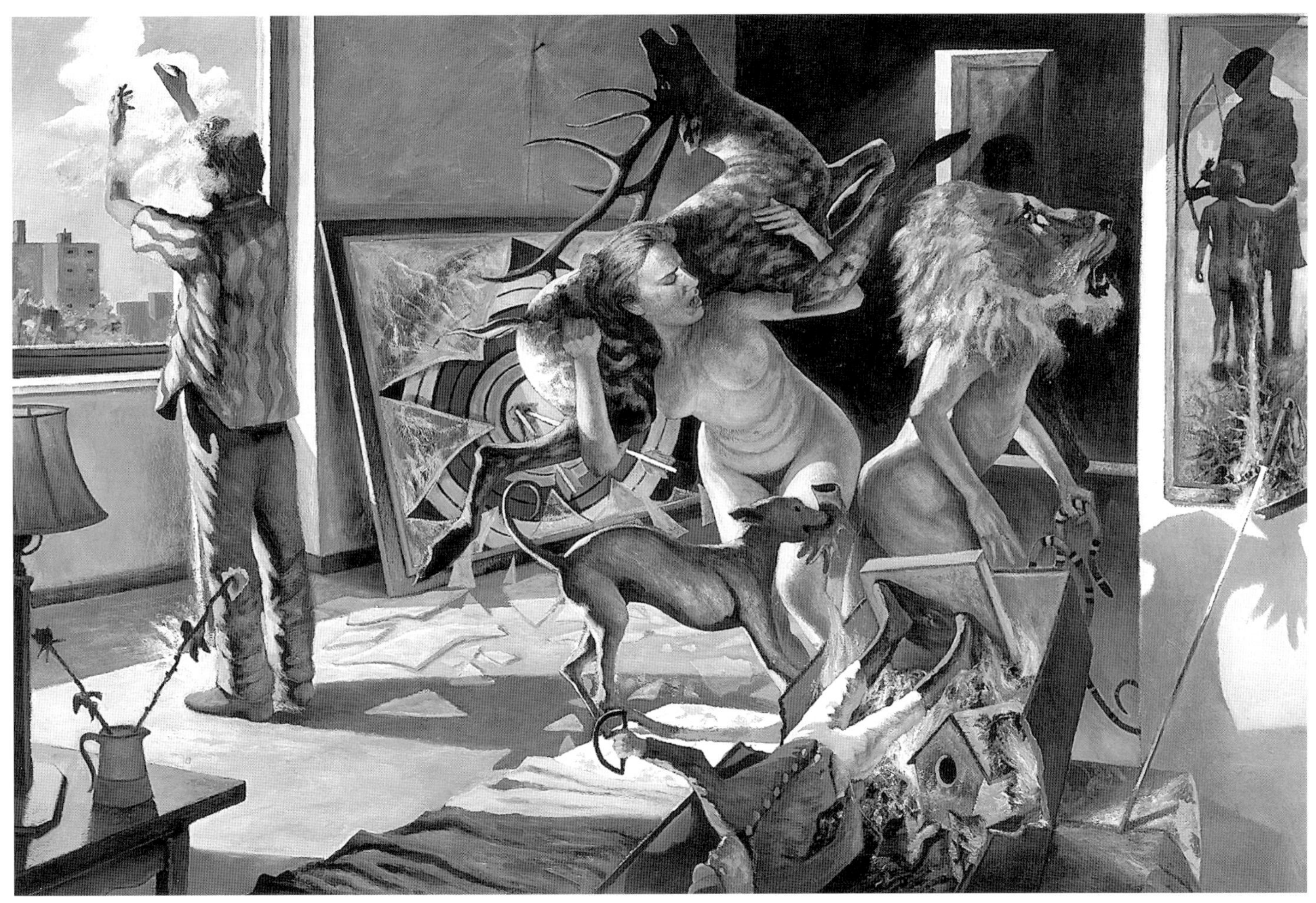

Untitled, 1994-95

CATALOGUE № 17

First Scene (1993-95, cat. no. 16) presents a clue in its punning title to Gustin's concentration on problems of perception. The figure of the child exploring the mysterious chest (for toys?) speaks of discovery and the first experience of things; that this experience comes about or is informed by evolving images is perhaps indicated by the hobby horse and the image of the stricken netted stag just behind it. In each instance, a human power is exerted over either nature itself or the image of it. The carpet upon which these objects and figures appear is partly rolled back, revealing a stream of water running beneath—perhaps the current or flux of existence beneath our fixed images of it. At the back, through a hole in a painting (or painted wall), a hand extends a lit candle. This illuminator of the scene is largely hidden by a negligee or similar item of women's clothing partially draped over a wire clothes hanger. This dress, which can signal gender, mood, action, and feeling, is an example of an image which, as a human construct based upon our own form, can be used to express important realities. The floral still life on a small table introduces the theme of nature arranged for the purposes of art, a theme which animates many of Gustin's works. The bold and fresh handling and vivid, reverberating color charge the scene with that sense of the visionary which, elementally, this work is about.

One does not feel that the presentation of Gustin's vision has been simply a matter of dreaming it up and then setting it down. Visible *pentimenti* and variations in texture reveal that the scene has evolved in the making of it, that the process of doing the painting is the process of discovering and inventing it, not just the execution of a previously held idea. In this way, Gustin firmly unites the practice of painting with its substance, content, and meaning. If his scenes seem to be part of some vast operatic-scale drama unfolded before us, it is one the artist is constantly composing. The act of painting is as much Gustin's subject or theme as any other, but the greatest understanding of his challenging work can come about only through realizing the ideas and states of feeling that inspire his activity as a painter. The fullness and even overflowing nature of his imagery suggest that his artistic awareness and temperament are of great dynamic complexity and that he is possessed by them just as much as he can direct them. This conscious revelation of inner life, its ungovernable operations, and complicated, uncomfortable aspects is itself an artistic function of major importance. —*D.A.*

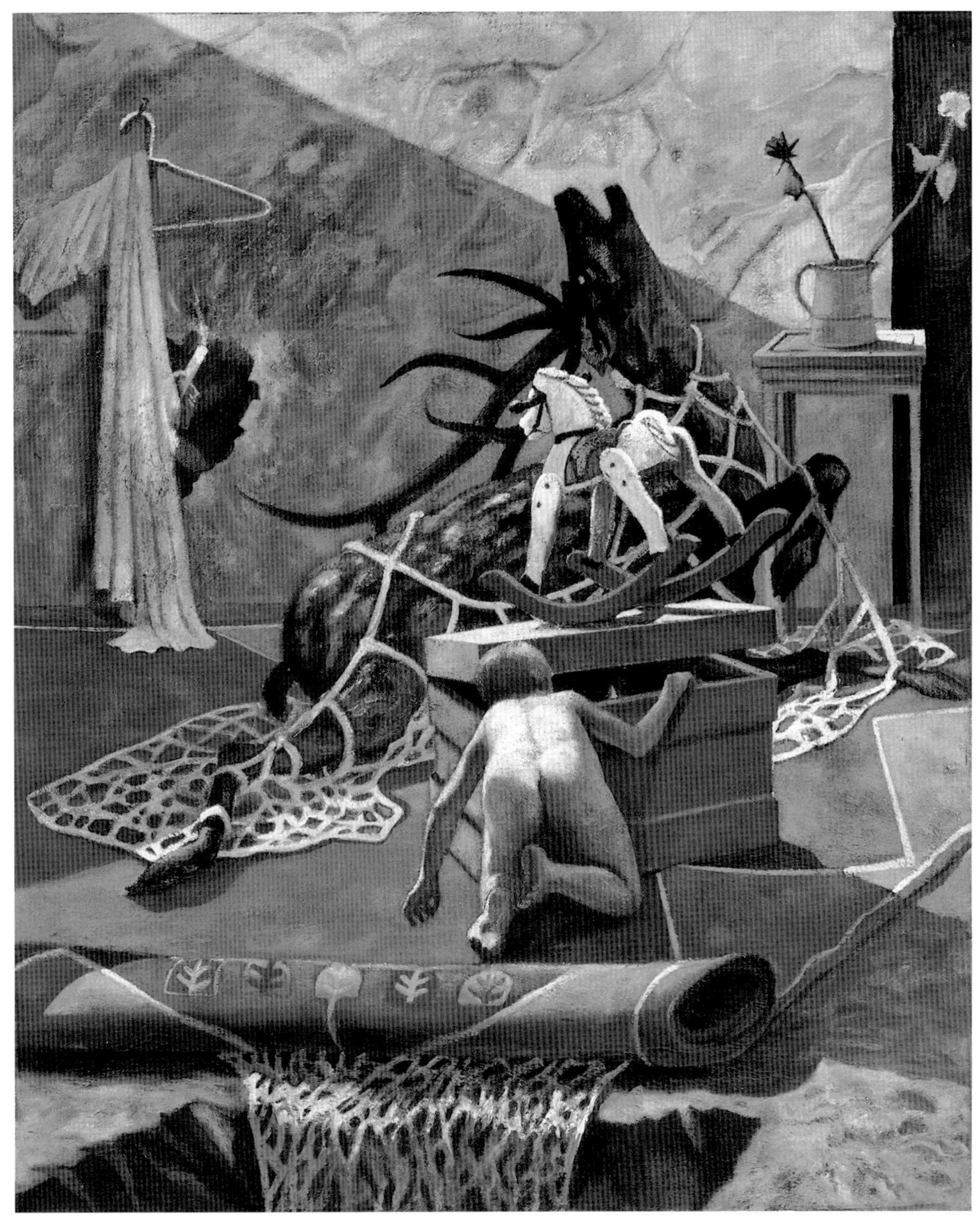

First Scene, 1993-95

MARK *jackson*

For over a decade and a half Mark Jackson's paintings have offered a wide-ranging exploration of figure-painting types and modalities along with a seemingly unending concern with rich, painterly handling. The works that first brought him notice were so heavily impastoed that they constituted a kind of *mezzo-relievo* in paint. Usually small and very sculptural, these works, instead of being built up in some modeling medium and then painted, were built up with paint itself, occasionally to several inches. One wonders whether pictures now fifteen and more years old will ever dry completely. From this extreme point, Jackson's surfaces rapidly became much thinner, though still exhibiting a vigorous impasto created with both brush and knife in large, bold strokes. One impetus to this comparatively more conventional use of pigment was the artist's move to larger formats and greater compositional and figural monumentality. The early, thick paintings had to be done on wood or masonite panels; as they became larger, their weight and maneuverability grew increasingly problematic. To get back onto more convenient canvas or linen, Jackson had to reduce the mass of paint.

Throughout this period, his pictures dealt with a strange blend of imagery wherein features of photographically derived magazine illustrations, advertising images, candid photographs, and figures recalling the staples of physique magazines and show-biz tabloids are combined with portrait likenesses of the artist's friends, models, and acquaintances. As the paintings grew larger (sometimes employing compound canvases), the scale of the figures increased to the gigantic; the effect is especially imposing when the figures do not fit entirely within the format. There is perhaps some relationship here to the gigantism of Alfred Leslie and Philip Pearlstein, but Jackson's figures, frequently in active poses and with intense expressions, also have about them a billboardlike feeling, partly due to his carefully chosen and usually restricted chromatic range. The paintings are both expressive and to a degree expressionistic, although Jackson never unleashes his brush- (or knife-) work to a degree that his strokes act in complete independence of their constructive and descriptive function in the image.

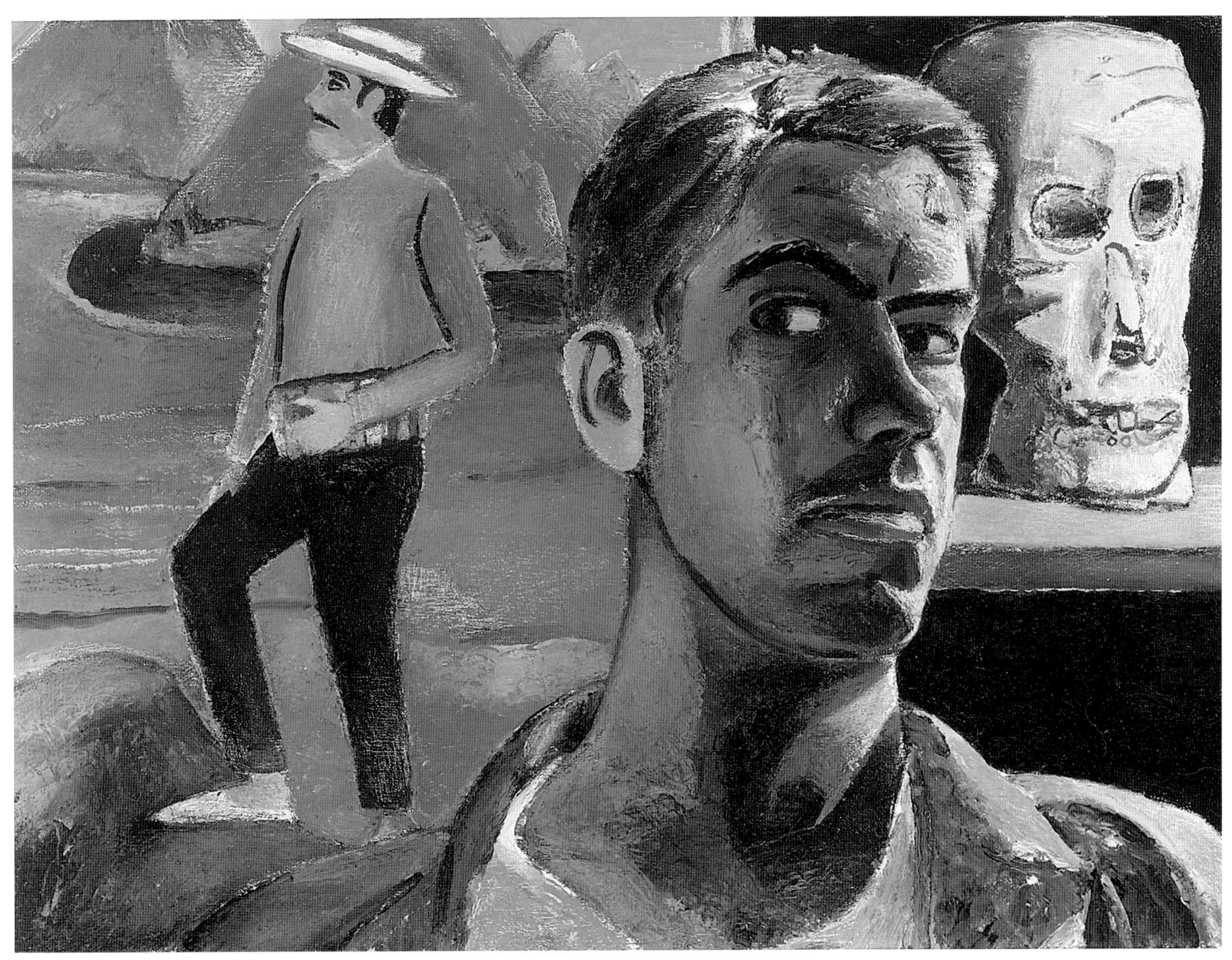

Self-Portrait, 1994

More recently, Jackson's formats have again become somewhat smaller, down to the range where his figural images, life size or a bit over, sit easily on them. He still frequently truncates the figures by the edge of the canvas, so the monumentality of his previous period is maintained in an effective (if altered) way. For the present, the related issues of scale and size in Jackson's work may be said to be at a kind of midpoint. From this position, a variety of interesting developments have ensued: now occasionally still-life and other kinds of accessories make up part of the image, inflecting its meaning. In the untitled reclining male nude of 1993 (cat. no. 20), the images in the background, the reflection of the model's bent leg in the mirror, and the somewhat uncomfortable-looking small bed on which the model lies all add to the atmosphere of tension and defiant confrontation created by the figure.

Jackson's relatively small (20 x 26 in.) *Self-Portrait* (1994, cat. no. 22) sets off the background images of a painting and a strange sculpture against the guarded and perhaps slightly sneering expression worn by the artist. Though we feel that he has certainly used the mirror for this picture, the effect he has created is like that of an unposed photograph or a still from a film sequence. We see not only what the artist looks like, but also what he looks like in a specific moment of feeling or action which we cannot grasp fully. The result is that we examine the images again and again, rather as we do when looking at the individually comprehensible motifs in René Magritte's mysterious (from a functional point of view) ensembles.

The sensibility put forth by Jackson's figures is, like Doud's, a bit unsettling. Forcing the figures up close, using a restricted palette and a sophisticated exploitation of tonal effects, Jackson articulates transient emotions or thoughts of which the sitter himself seems not entirely aware—and which are not necessarily benign. This air of threat or menace in Jackson's work comes directly from his apprehension of contemporary society as pervaded with danger, anxiety, and clashes of feeling. It is of the greatest interest that Jackson has elected to exploit the forms and techniques of grand-manner painting in order to show us the present. By doing so, he both underlines the validity of this kind of artistic statement in the past and asserts his conviction that it is of great relevance to our understanding the experience of the present. —D.A.

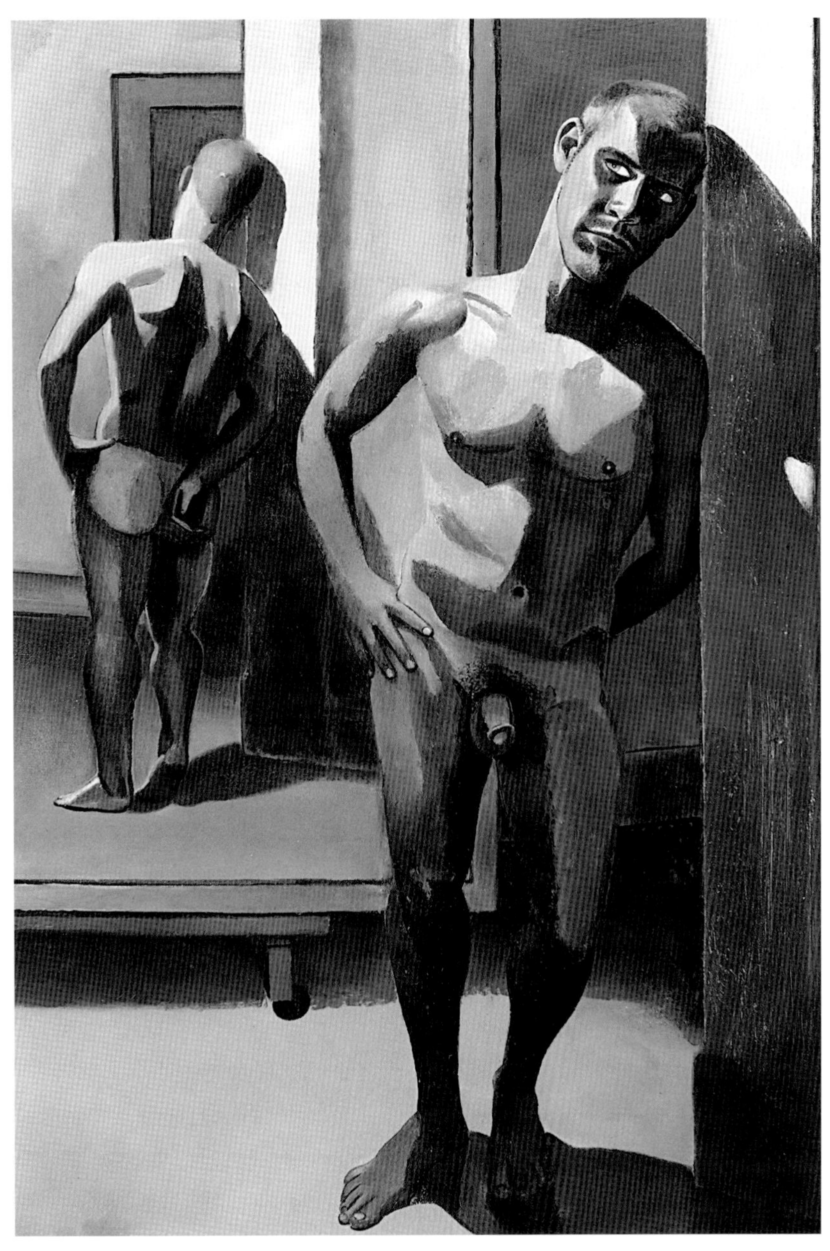

Standing Nude, 1995

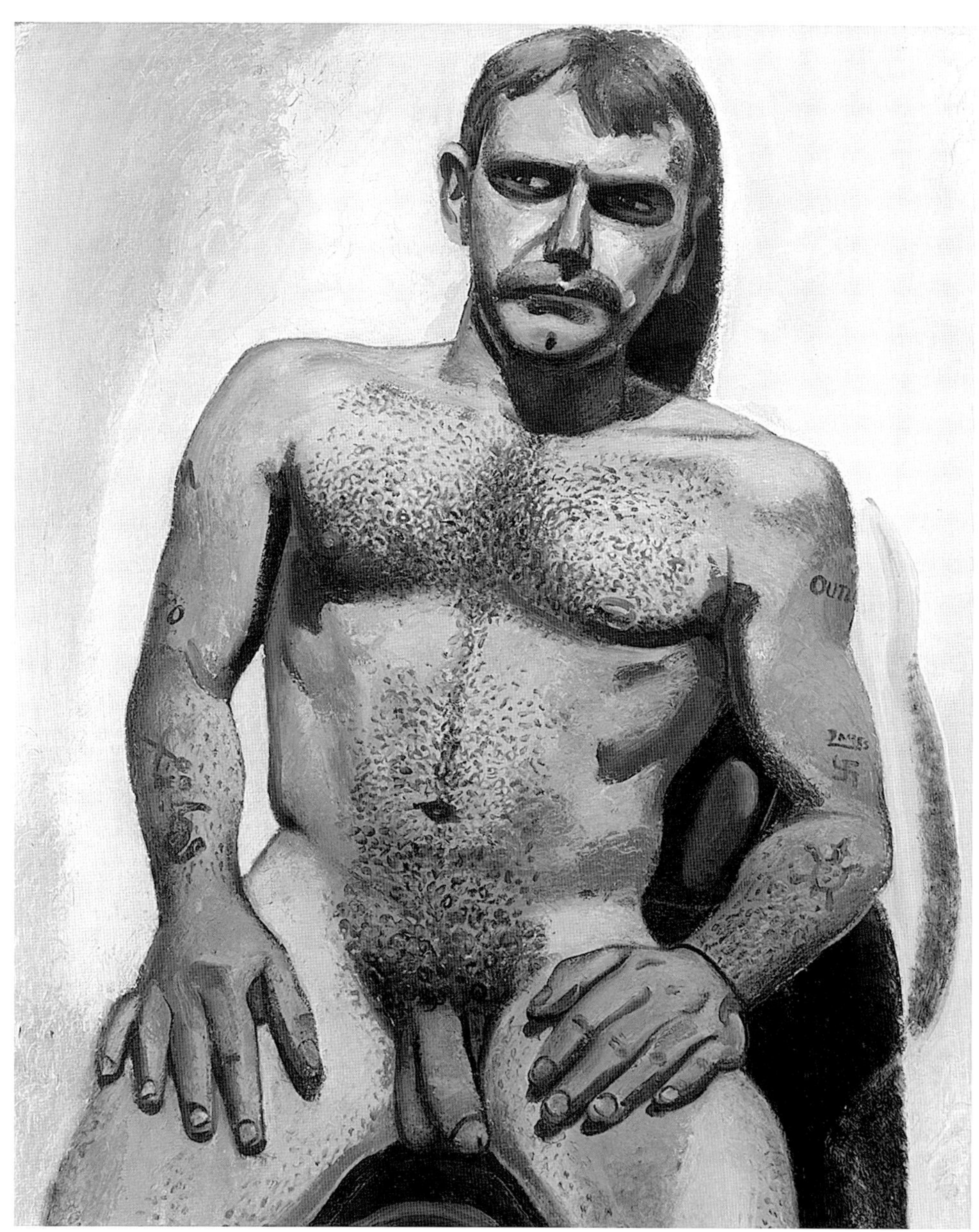

Untitled (Seated Nude), 1992

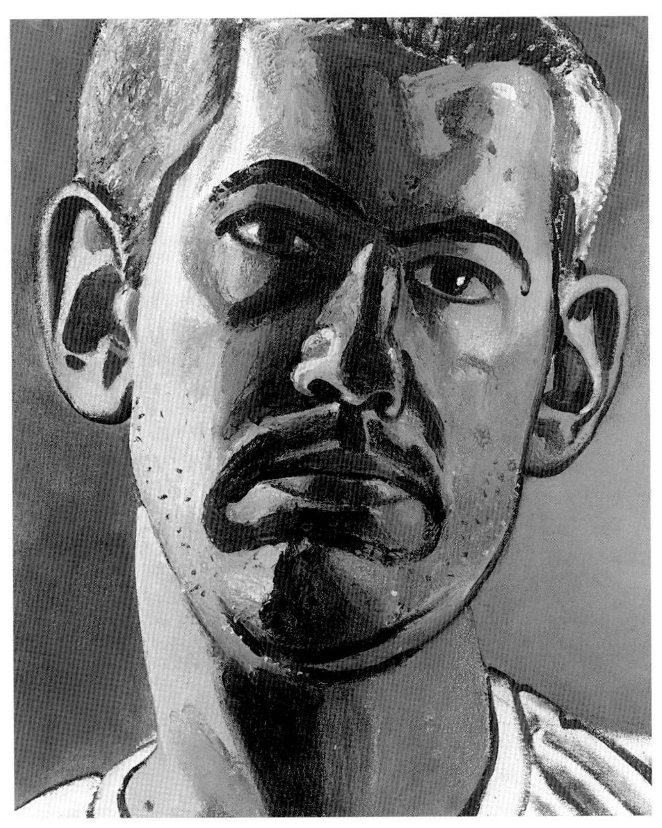

Self-Portrait, 1993

CATALOGUE № 19

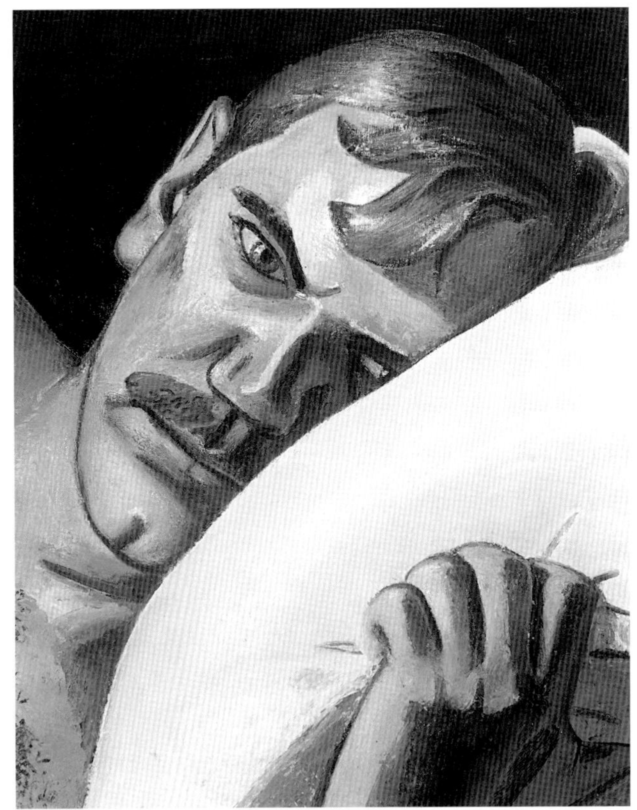

Untitled, 1993

CATALOGUE № 21

ROBERT *lucy*

The distinctive, slightly unsettling nature of many of Robert Lucy's paintings connects him with a current of strangeness in such artists as James Ensor, Balthus, and, to a certain extent, René Magritte. This oddity of the ordinary, so to speak, is partly the result of a deep perception, beyond the customary aim of functional identification, in which the forms and colors of things can and do give rise to whole other universes of possible significance and chains of associative meanings. This kind of experience can also spring from a special concentration on the orderliness of construction, the visual rhythms of pictorial architecture, and the nearly indescribable, mysterious affinities we sense exist between and among images and objects. For example, this feeling of a magical order arising out of a deep perception of reality is the wonderful hallmark of Piero della Francesca, whose timeless sense of an unalterable actuality comes not from faithfulness to observational detail but from an understanding of harmonic relationships and structural integrity of form, which is the artist's way of seeing.

Lucy's work often combines such structural considerations and experiences of form with more subjective emotional elements. These are the psychological aspects of both the artist's own nature and perception and of his responses to people and things. His diamond-shaped *Self-Portrait* (1995, cat. no. 30) presents the artist's bust-length likeness, his features concentrated and alert, against a composition of verticals and horizontals which alludes directly to the formal schemes of Piet Mondrian and Theo Van Doesburg. The only diagonals *within* the composition are formed by a bit of the molding above a doorway and by the angles of the canvas itself reflected in the mirror. The whole image is a mirror reflection, something made inescapably clear only by this one not very conspicuous detail. What happens here is just what occurs in Lucy's constructivist forebears: the diagonal edges of the canvas are given a compositional prominence and variety of function not always apparent in the usual rectangular painting format. While we certainly react emotionally to the figurative image before us, the artist presents himself in a severely formal context. Accordingly, the absolute centrality of his nose in the design, the color and placement of the single

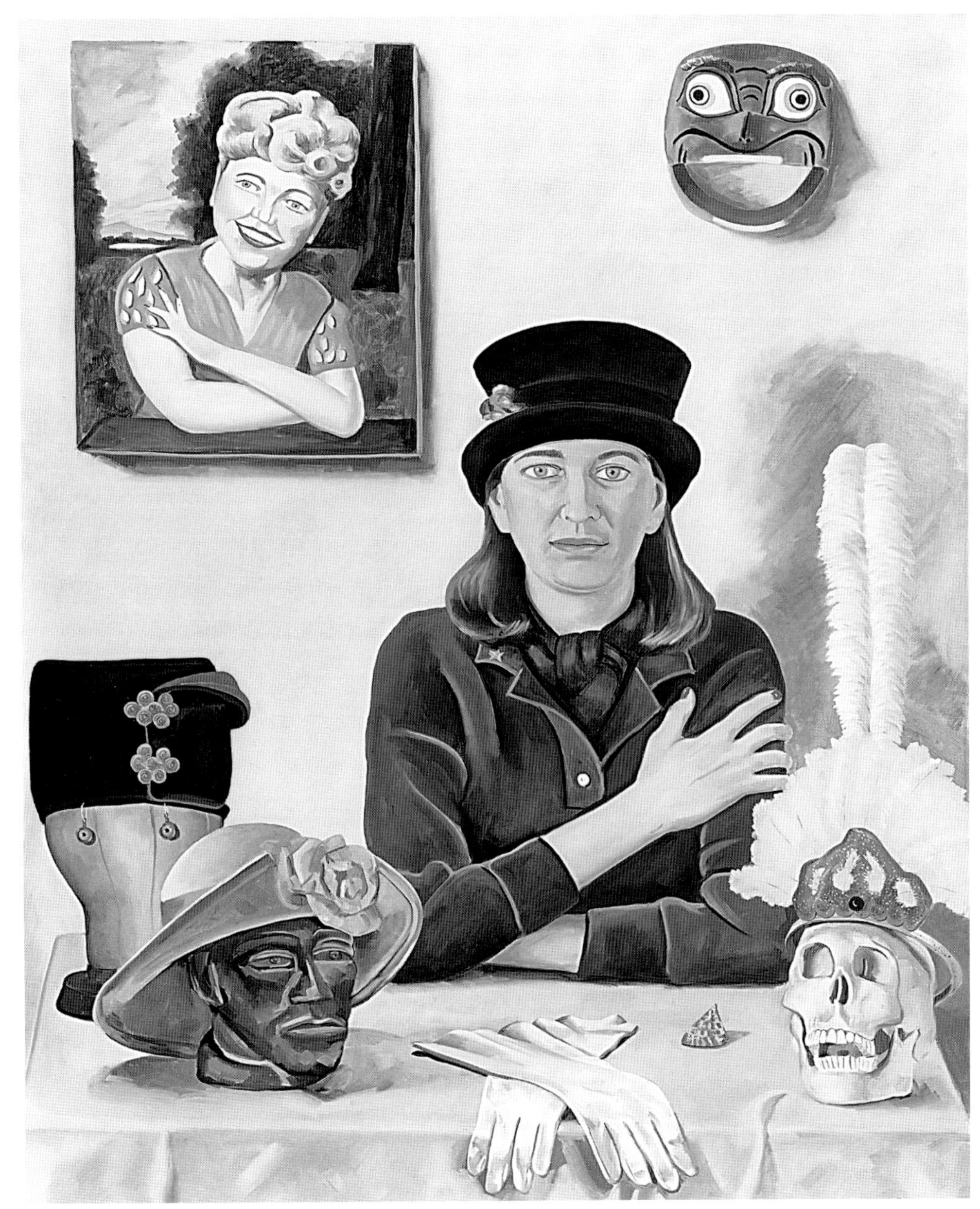

Laura with Hats, 1993

CATALOGUE № 26

shirt-pocket button, lead us to apprehend other "natural" aspects of the image—the folds of the shirt, the levels of the pockets, even certain facial details—as equally significant in a purely formal way to the more obvious structural elements. This is perhaps the key to one of the important ways Lucy would like us to look at his work.

Lucy's wonderful *Portrait of Sylvia Sleigh* (1995, cat. no. 29), like most of his other works, sets out following a well established pictorial category, the full-length standing portrait. The picture's many allusive aspects are inseparably woven together within its formal structure. The subject appears in her sitting room which, significantly, is the setting in many of her own compositions—nudes, portraits, and nude portraits. Sleigh's beautiful dress, quizzing expression, and interesting posture, relaxed yet ready to dart into movement, are indications of her own nature and even her approach to painting. Her work, like this portrait, blends formality and candid observation and often includes details, such as the cats in Lucy's picture, which may seem gratuitous but which turn out to be essential in subtle inflections of both mood and composition. For example, the curvatures of the cats' tails in this picture rhyme with the curves of the mirror frame, the arch of the fireplace opening, and the arc of the tondo portrait of Lawrence Alloway (Sleigh's late husband) in the upper left.

The painting is honorific: Sleigh is an artist whom Lucy greatly admires and he includes her work here, both the tondo portrait and a section of her huge room-painting *Invitation to a Voyage* (begun in 1983) seen reflected in the overmantel mirror. The pose, among other things, is that of "posing for one's portrait," becoming the subject of artistic consideration, and the homage is completed by the inclusion of Lucy's partial self-portrait image, also reflected in the mirror. In coloring and delicacy of handling, this portrait makes additional references to Sleigh as an artist; the sprightly animation and energetic presence her image puts forth also gives weight to her personality. In a way, this image can be said to operate as a kind of muse for the entire exhibition: most of the artists are well aware of Sleigh's work and acknowledge its importance to them in various ways—quite a few of them visible in the works shown here, as in the present instance. —*D.A.*

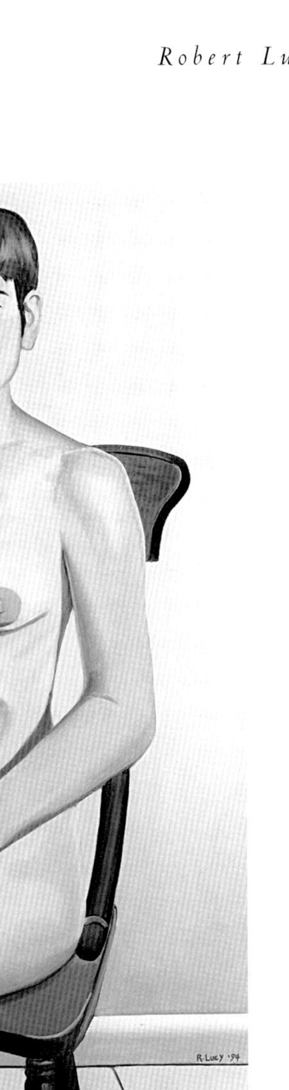

The Mesmerist, 1994

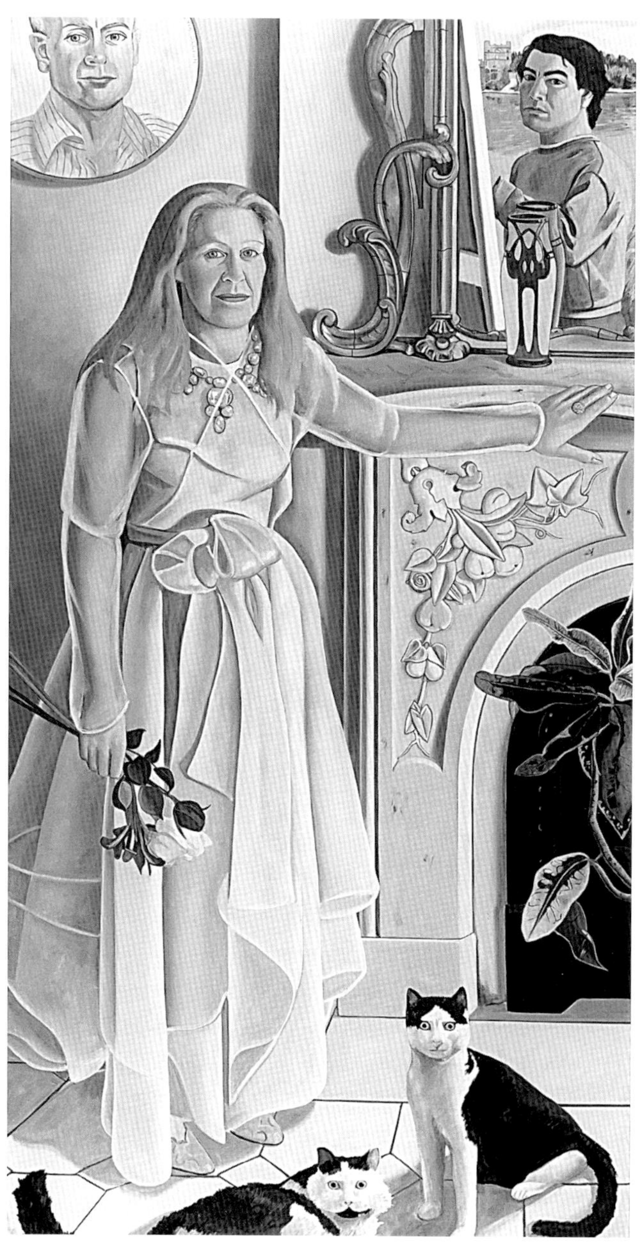

Portrait of Sylvia Sleigh, 1995

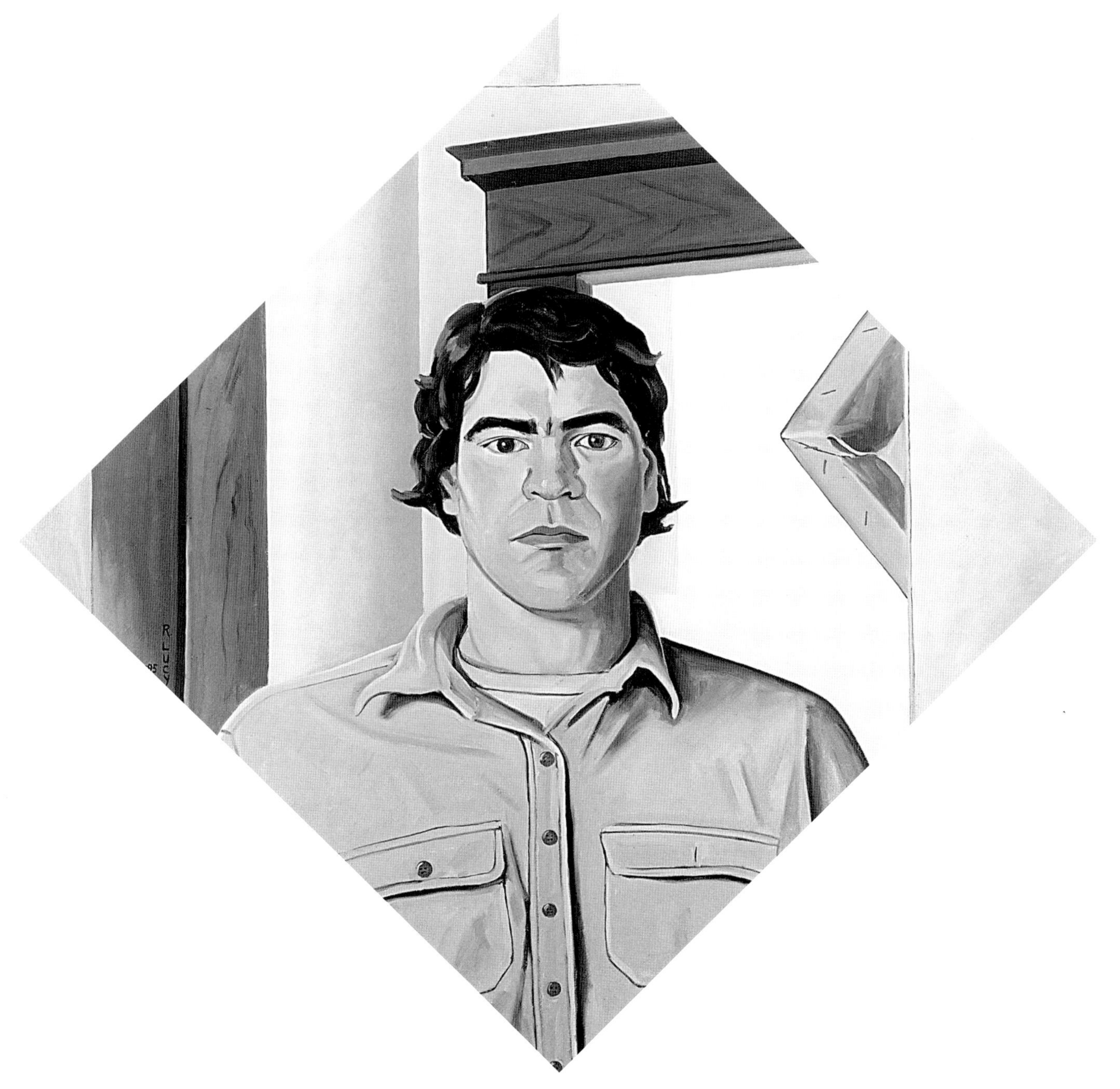

Self-Portrait, 1995

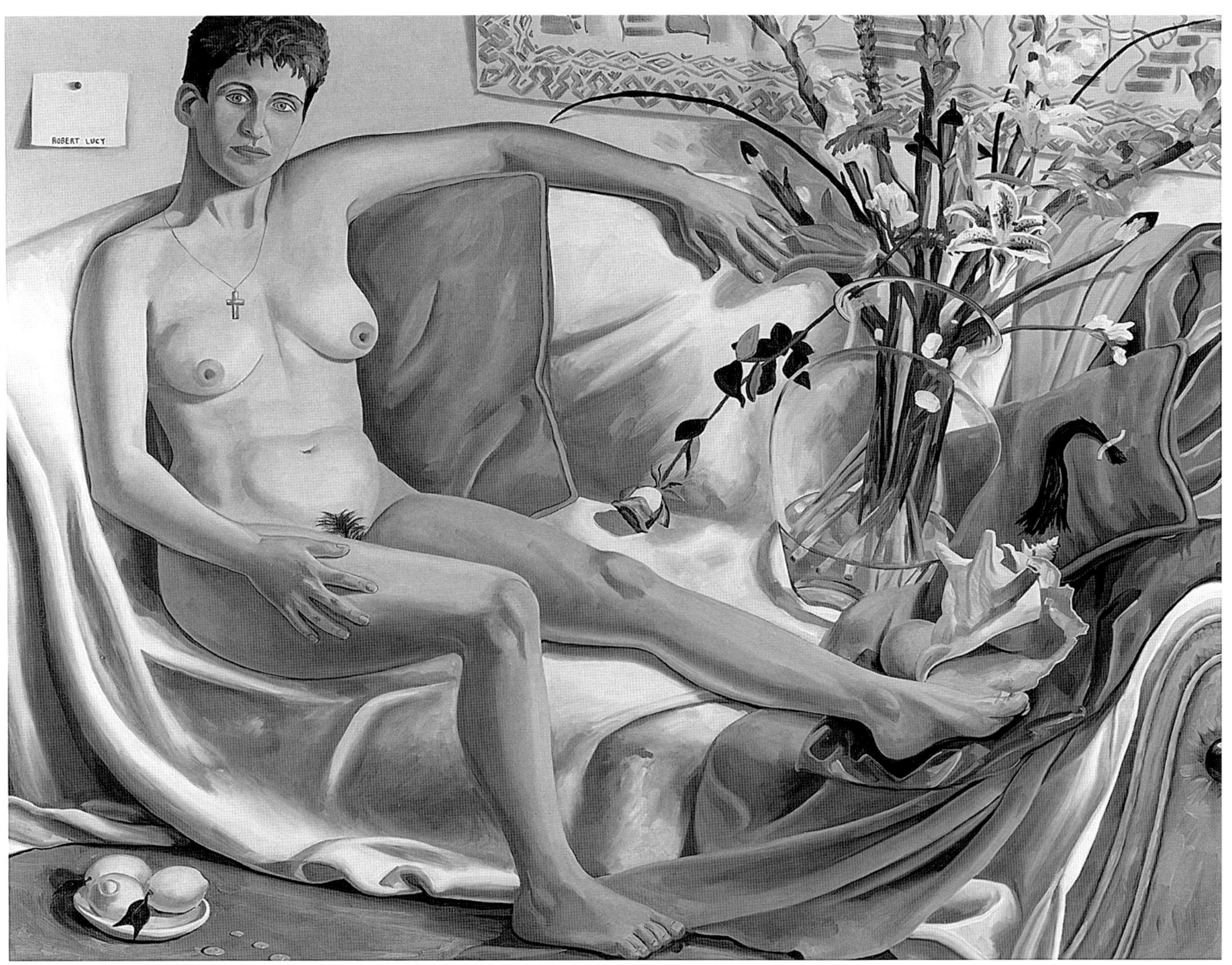

Reclining Nude with Flowers, 1992

CATALOGUE № 24

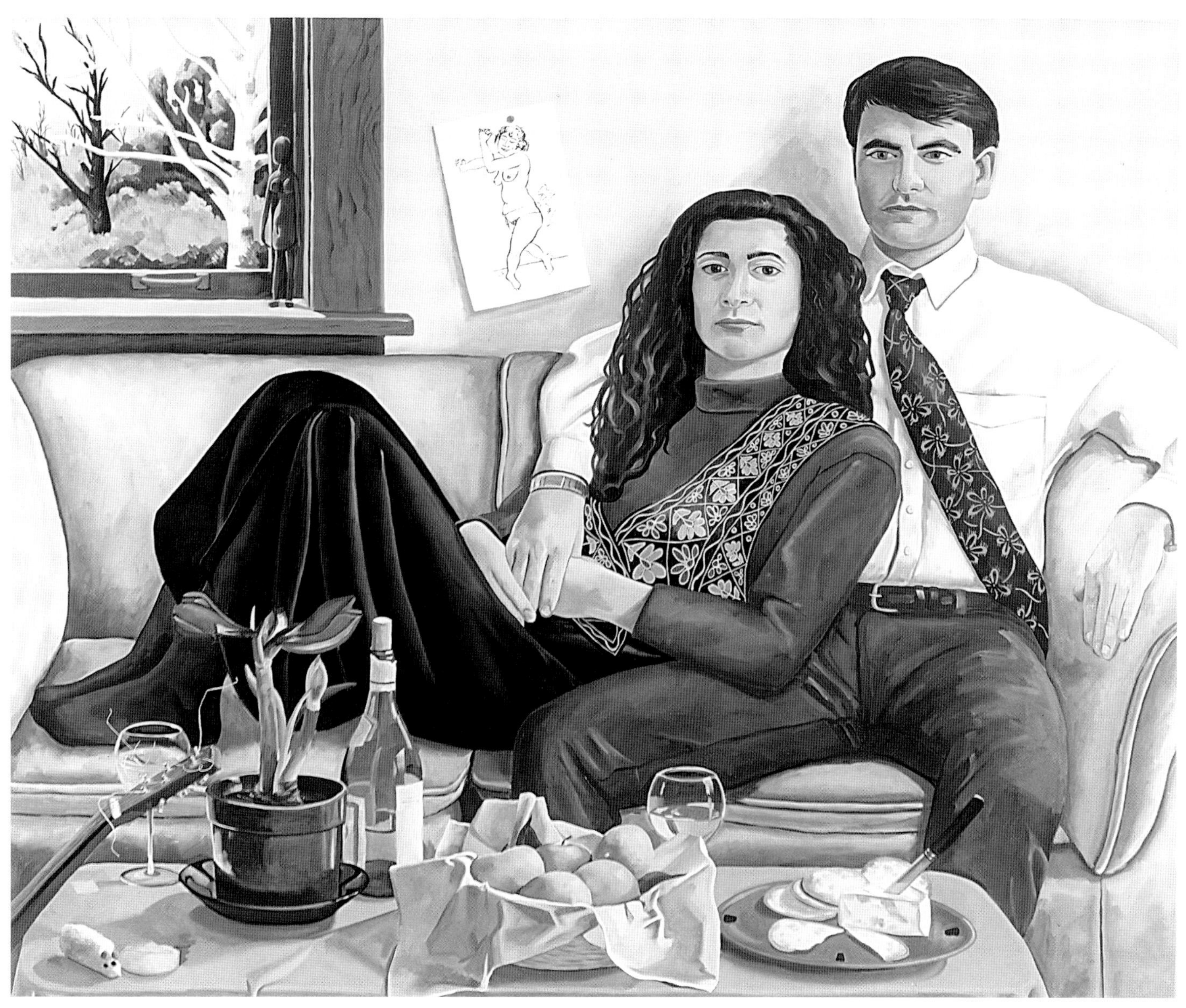

Stephanie D'Alessandro and David Rownd, 1993

RICHARD *willenbrink*

Richard Willenbrink's paintings have a very forthright engagement with the Grand Manner through their handling, high-key color, life-size figure scale, and the dynamic compositional roles given to the nude singly and in groups. He also tackles themes from myth, legend, and even religious history which have long been core grand-manner subjects. In keeping with many of his forebears, Willenbrink takes up such themes not only because the subjects or stories are interesting, curious, or provocative in themselves but also *principally* because they can be used to frame a variety of metaphysical points of view, ranging from moralistic reflections to considerations of the nature and function of art.

The narrative represented in *The Flaying of Marsyas* (1993, cat. no. 33) traditionally warns against art's competition with divine creation, admonishing that the artist's function is to manifest and acknowledge the nature of reality, not to rival it. The cruel punishment of the satyr who presumed to challenge Apollo to a contest of musical skill refers to the inescapable consequences of exalting one's own powers over those of the universal realities of which they are but products. Also, of course, the subject offers a wonderful opportunity to show two male nudes in action other than a battle, sporting, or bathing scene. Both the actions and poses of the figures are in opposition, allowing for contrasts of form and feeling: the captive satyr writhes and winces, while the god coolly begins the flaying with the calm deliberation of a taxidermist. Apollo reveals in the most vivid and horrific way that we are flesh and cannot escape our imprisonment within its envelope except by death. That this subject is also the theme of Titian's last great painting, a masterwork recently shown in this country and well known to Willenbrink, is relevant here: does Willenbrink risk playing Marsyas to Titian's Apollo?

There are further traditional meanings in the subject: Marsyas's pipe-playing is considered inferior to the harmonic, geometrically linked, and chordal structures of Apollo's instrument, the lyre; the lyre player, moreover, can accompany his music with song while the wind performer cannot. The forms of music have long been regarded as paradigmatic of relationships

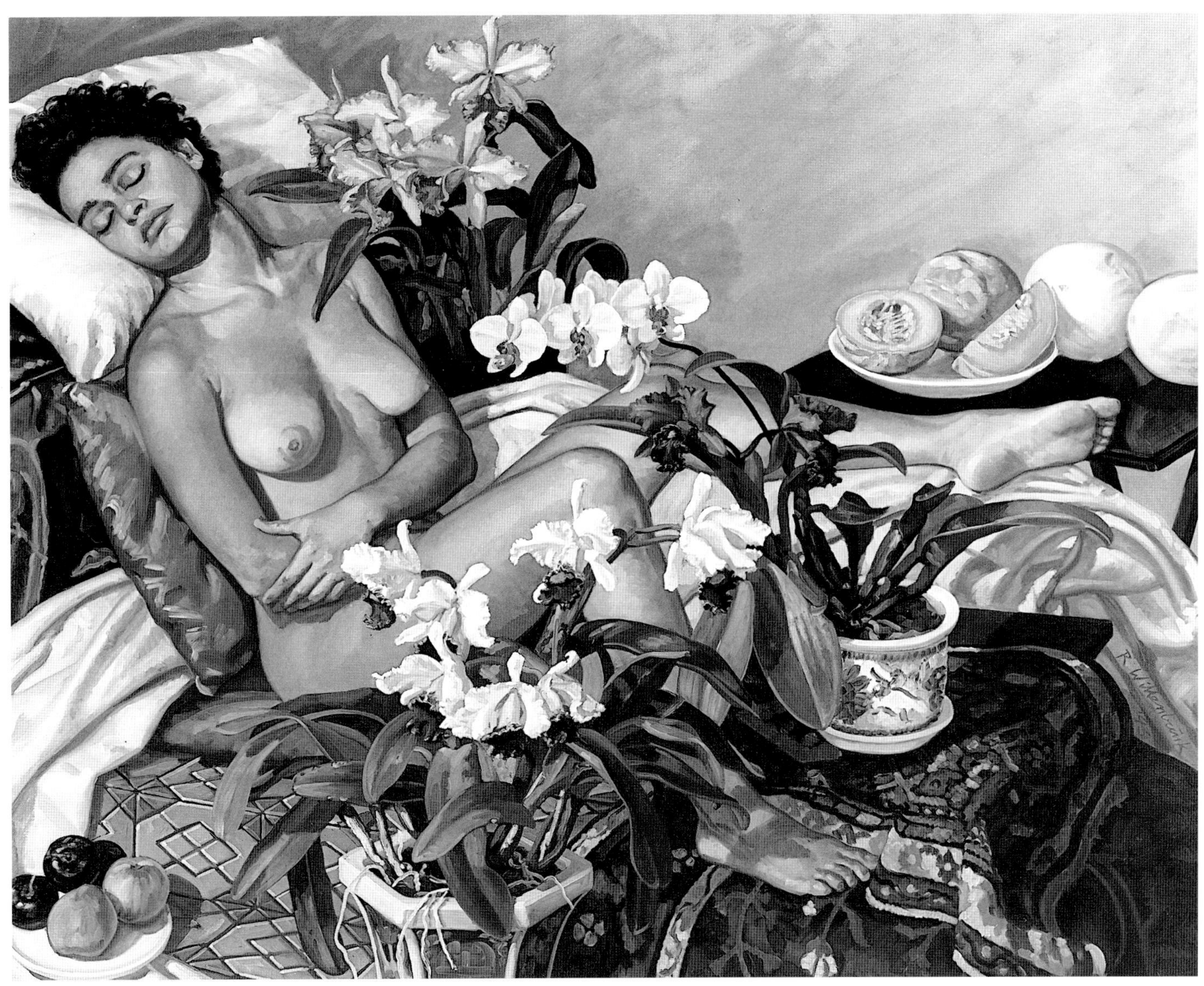

Orchidelirium, 1993

CATALOGUE № 34

within various kinds of artistic compositions—partly because music is not physical but relational and while it can be notated, there remains the question whether and in what sense musical notation is music itself. Just as the visual arts may be a kind of notation of another connected reality, their precise relationship to that reality is an involved question.

Willenbrink's *Salome* (1992, cat. no. 32) is concerned with an equally complicated series of issues. Salome is the subject of many important works of art from Donatello's bronze relief of *The Feast of Herod* (1433-35) to Richard Strauss's 1905 opera and to a number of films. Strauss's *Salome* itself is based closely on Oscar Wilde's play of 1893, which was a *succès de scandale* in its time (as was the opera). Salome is a vexing subject: its problematic aspect has been focused on anew by feminist criticism. Is she a classic example of the adolescent female as an exploitee of the predatory male gaze, that is, as a *femme fatale* whose seemingly unbridled erotic interest in the Baptist is both attractive and monstrous?

In both Wilde's play and Strauss's opera, Herodias's daughter, Salome, has been perverted by her mother, abused in fact, in order to provide an object of libidinous desire for Herod (her brother-in-law and husband and thus Salome's uncle) for the purposes of consolidating and maintaining Herodias's own influential position at the Judaean court. The depravity of Herod's rather incestuous appetite is horrible, balanced by the ruination of Salome's potential as a woman by the precocious awakening and cultivation of her sexuality by others for their own ends. She has been grossly victimized in a dysfunctional family; and her tragedy is that despite her attraction to a figure holding the promise of spiritual healing (the Baptist), as still a child of about fifteen she is able to approach him only through her forced, hot-house sexuality—which the Baptist must reject. (He is onto her unknowing role as her mother's cat's paw.) Because Salome's most important human aspect, her capacity for a spiritual (not necessarily religious) life, is deformed or stifled, she has been robbed of even the ability to save herself through what the Baptist represents. She has been cheated of the possibility of a life, and the wings of the shadow of death, mentioned in Wilde's text and Strauss's libretto, darken one of the walls in Willenbrink's interior.

Willenbrink's employment of the mirror in this subject introduces the note of mental reflection on the significance of the subject—after all, Salome cannot see this reflection, but we can. Her attention is on the head of the Baptist and the loss of the possibility of redeeming her own integrity as a human being. The cautionary content for the artist is not to permit the sensual to stunt or prevent the development of the spiritual, philosophical, and metaphysical, that is, to ensure that the aim of art is compassionate wisdom and pleasure in it and not sensual gratification alone. —*D.A.*

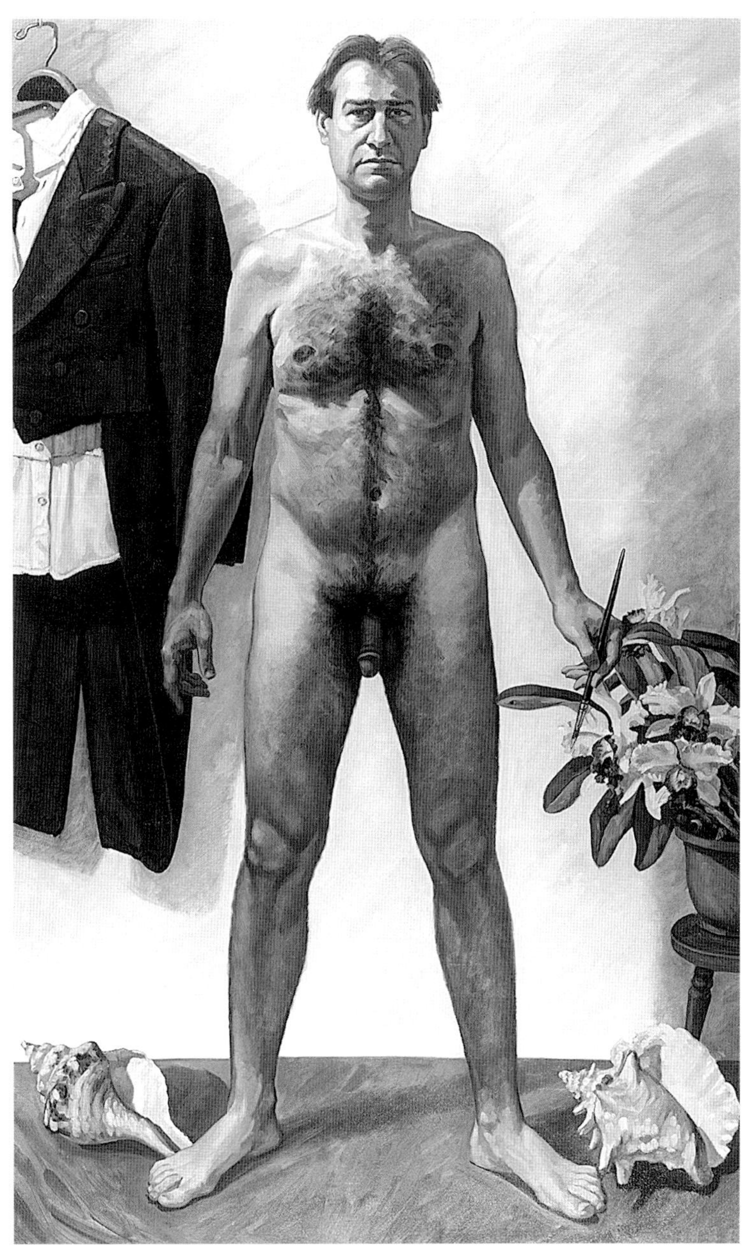

Nude Self-Portrait, 1995

CATALOGUE № 35

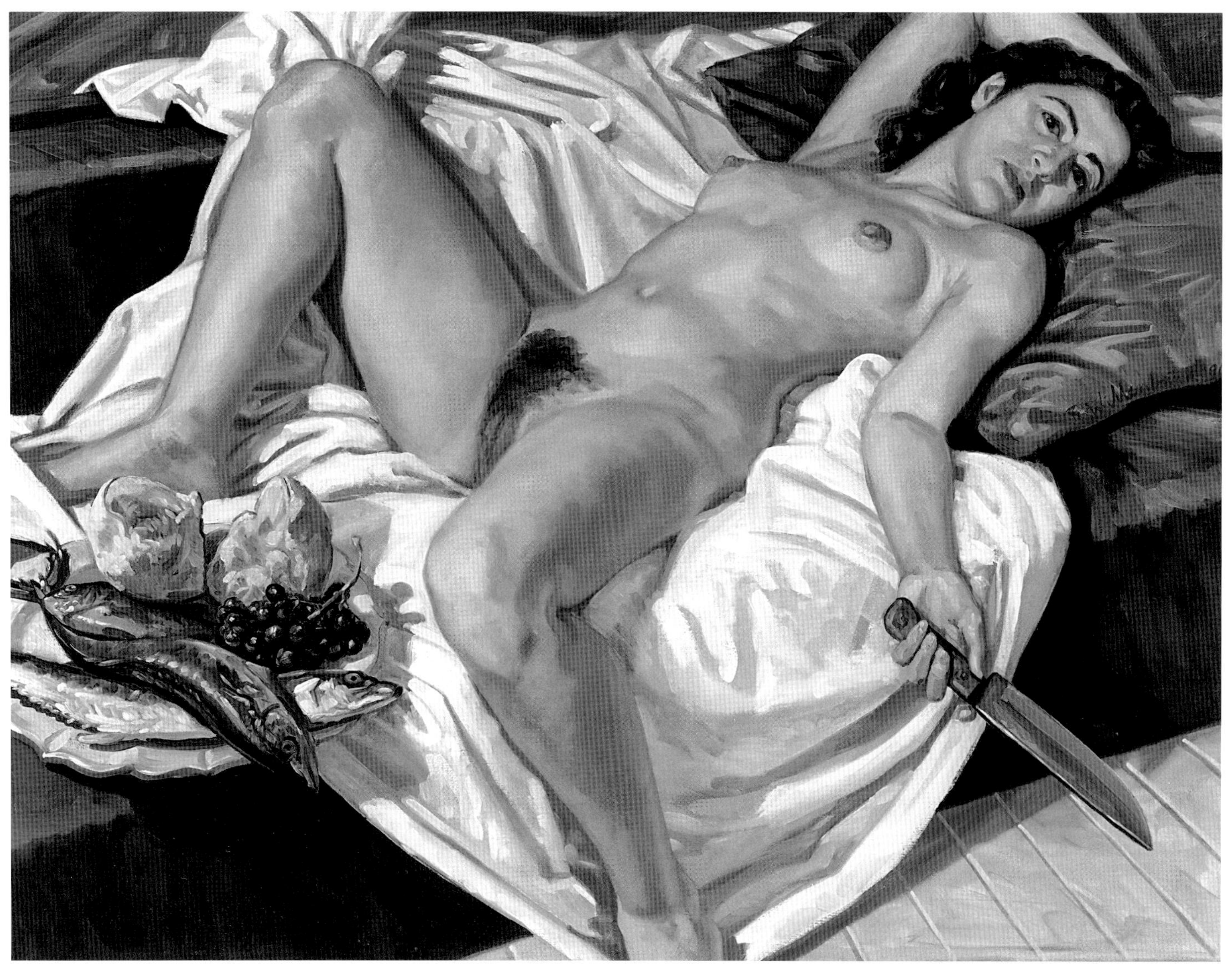

Nude with a Knife, 1991

CATALOGUE №31

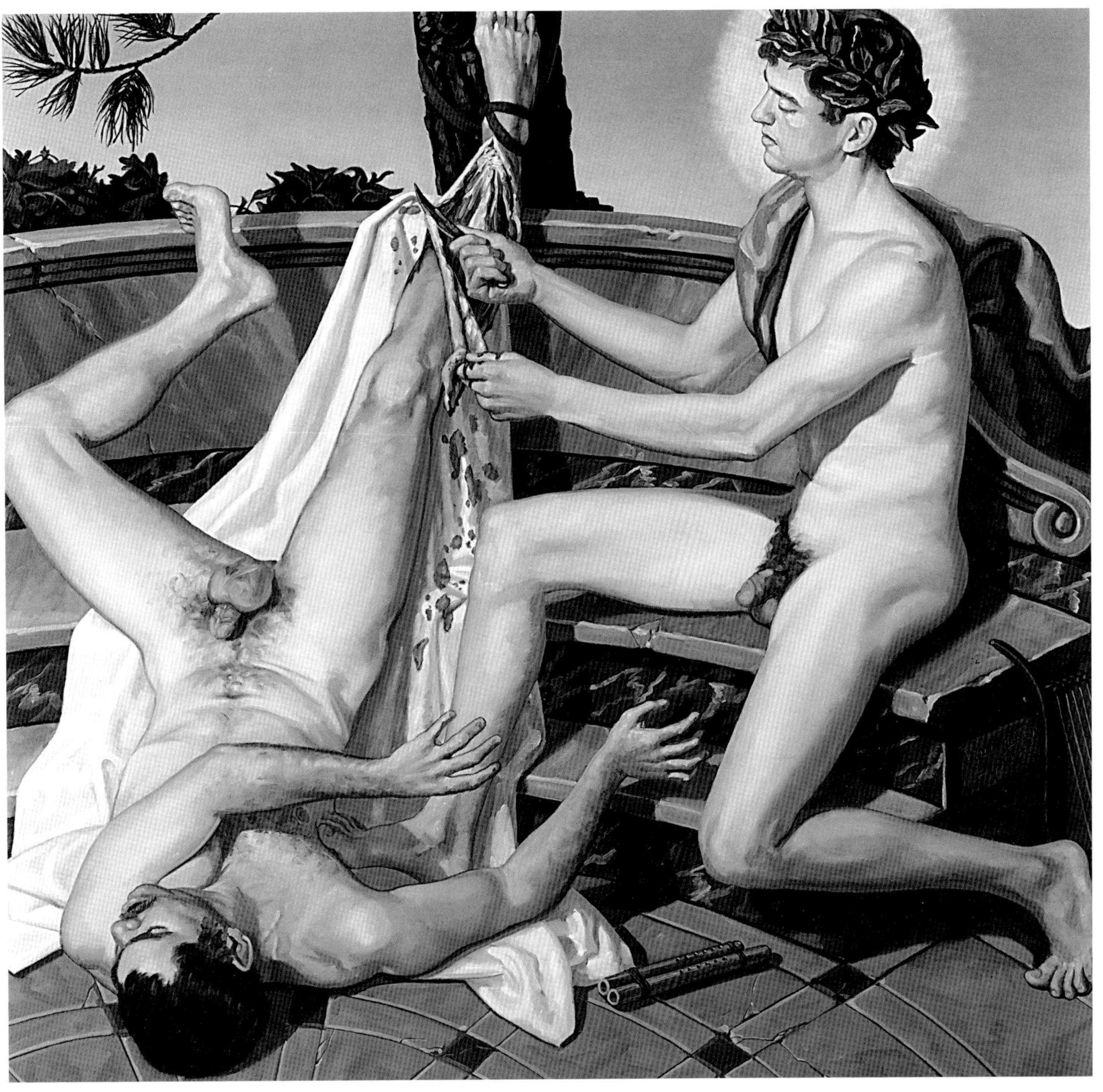

The Flaying of Marsyas, 1993

CATALOGUE № 33

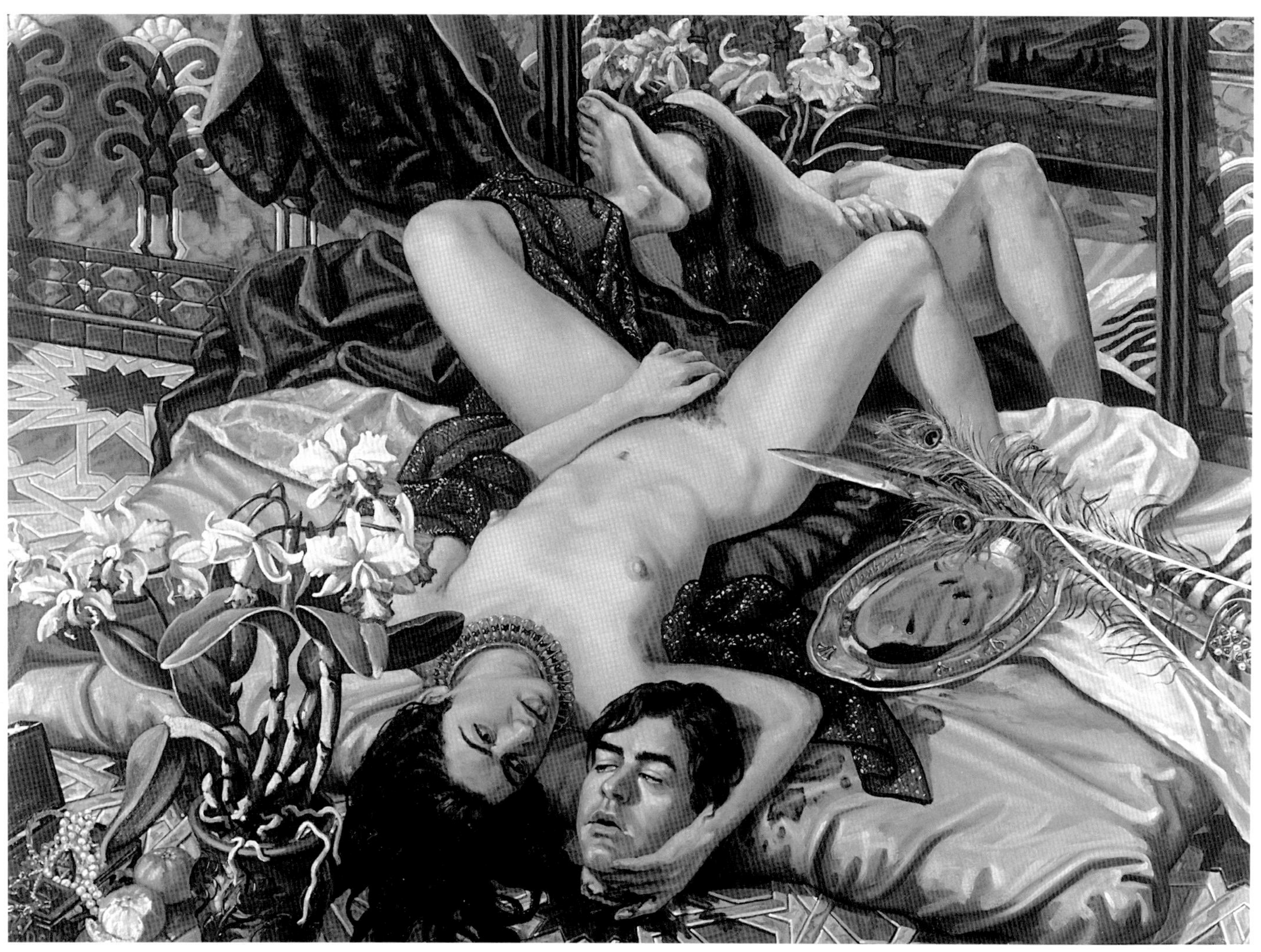

Salome, 1992

CATALOGUE № 32

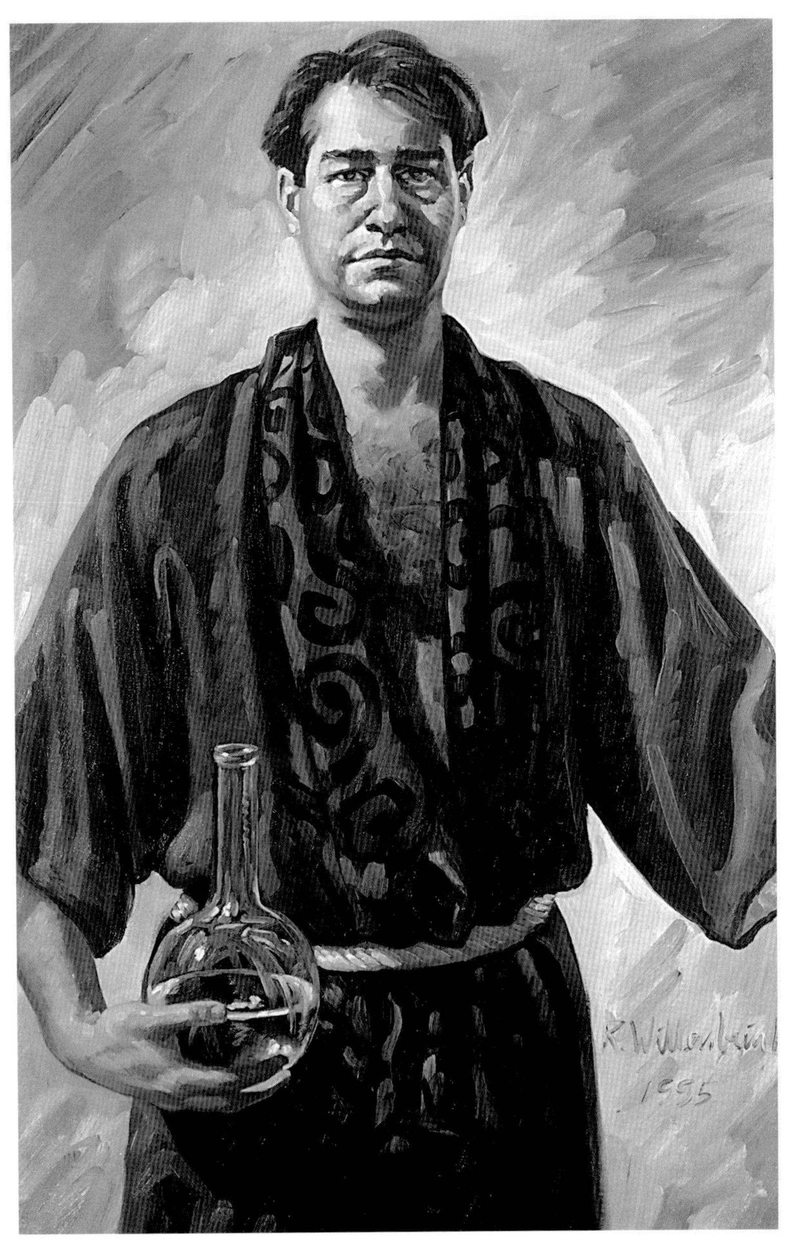

Self-Portrait in a Red Robe, 1995

CATALOGUE № 37

ANNE ABRONS

Born New York, 1950
B.A., Bennington College, Vermont, 1972

Exhibition Checklist

1. *Annette Maryan in My Studio,* 1990
   Oil on linen
   48 x 42 in. (121.9 x 106.7 cm)
   Courtesy of Sonia Zaks Gallery, Chicago

2. *David: Night Portrait,* 1992
   Oil on linen
   24 x 36 in. (61.0 x 91.4 cm)
   Courtesy of Sonia Zaks Gallery, Chicago

3. *Double Ondine,* 1992
   Oil on linen
   40 x 34 in. (101.6 x 86.4 cm)
   Courtesy of Sonia Zaks Gallery, Chicago

4. *Family Portrait,* 1993
   Oil on linen
   60 x 36 in. (152.4 x 91.4 cm)
   Courtesy of Sonia Zaks Gallery, Chicago

5. *Seated Model in the Studio,* 1993
   Oil on linen
   54 x 42 in. (137.1 x 106.7 cm)
   Courtesy of Sonia Zaks Gallery, Chicago

6. *Ken in Gay Pride Parade Costume,* 1994
   Oil on linen
   60 x 48 in. (152.4 x 121.9 cm)
   Courtesy of Sonia Zaks Gallery, Chicago

7. *Nude Self-Portrait,* 1995
   Oil on linen
   60 x 48 in. (152.4 x 121.9 cm)
   Courtesy of Sonia Zaks Gallery, Chicago

8. *Robert Lucy in My Studio,* 1995
   Oil on linen
   60 x 48 in. (152.4 x 121.9 cm)
   Lent by Keith Hartley, Edinburgh

Individual Exhibitions

1990, 1988, 1985

Ruth Siegel Gallery, New York

1981

Anne Abrons: Paintings of the Human Figure,
Suzanne Lemberg Usdan Gallery,
Bennington College, Vermont

Selected Group Exhibitions

1995

*Flora: Contemporary Artists and
the World of Flowers,* Leigh Yawkey Woodson
Art Museum, Wausau, Wisconsin (traveled
to Art Museum of Southeast Texas,
Beaumont; New Mexico Museum of
Natural History and Science, Albuquerque;
Gibbes Museum of Art, Charleston, South
Carolina; Dixon Gallery and Gardens,
Memphis through 1996)

1994

AHI Gallery, New York

The Human Condition, Greater Lafayette
Museum of Art, Lafayette, Indiana

1993

Interior Outlook, The Gallery at Hastings-
on-Hudson, New York

A Moment Becomes Eternity: Flowers,
Bergen Museum of Art and Science,
Paramus, New Jersey

1992

Anne Abrons–David Sharpe: The Four Seasons,
Michael Walls Gallery, New York

1991

Still Alive: Contemporary Still Life,
Rockford College Art Museum, Illinois

1990

Five from Bennington, Krasdale Foods Art
Gallery, New York

Regarding Art: Artworks about Art, John Michael
Koehler Arts Center, Sheboygan, Wisconsin

1989

New Still Life, Evanston Art Center, Illinois

Dennis Adrian: A Critical Subject, Struve
Gallery, Chicago

Still Objective Paintings, Fay Gold Gallery,
Atlanta

1988

West/Art and the Law, Toronto (traveled)

1986

Square and..., Ruth Siegel Gallery, New York

Painting and Sculpture Today 1986, Indianapolis
Museum of Art

Olympus Revisited, Summit Art Center,
New Jersey

Betsy Rosenfield Gallery, Chicago

The Object Revitalized, Paine Art Center and
Arboretum, Oshkosh, Wisconsin

1985

Harvest, Ruth Siegel Gallery, New York

Looking at Men, Artemisia Gallery, Chicago

Betsy Rosenfield Gallery, Chicago

1984

Salvo, Ruth Siegel Gallery, New York

Mythology and Religion in Recent Art, N.A.M.E. Gallery, Chicago

Observations: Four Realist Painters, N.A.M.E. Gallery, Chicago

1 + 1 = 2, Bernice Steinbaum Gallery, New York (traveled)

1983

Nocturne, Ruth Siegel Gallery, New York

Looking at Women, Artemisia Gallery, Chicago

Selected Women Painters, Castle Gallery, College of New Rochelle, New York

1982

Ten Variations on a Theme: The Human Figure, Ruth Siegel Gallery, New York

Selections from the Dennis Adrian Collection, Museum of Contemporary Art, Chicago

Realist Paintings: People and the Things in Women's Lives, Marymount-Manhattan College, New York

1978

7" x 9", N.A.M.E. Gallery, Chicago

1977

Art in Public Places, Organization of Independent Artists, New York

Bibliography

Adrian, Dennis. *New Still Life.* Evanston, Illinois: Evanston Art Center, 1989.

Bonesteel, Michael. "New Life for Still Life." *Pioneer Press Newspaper*, 28 September 1989.

Garver, Thomas H. "Flowers and the Spheres of Life: Some Personal Thoughts about Artists and Flowers" and "Anne Abrons." In *Flora: Contemporary Artists and the World of Flowers.* Wausau, Wisconsin: Leigh Yawkey Woodson Art Museum, 1995.

Hixson, Kathryn. "New Still Life." *Arts Magazine* 64:4 (December 1989): 105-6.

Holg, Garrett. "New Still Life [at] Evanston Art Center." *New Art Examiner* 17:5 (January 1990): 41-42.

Kind, Joshua. "Mythology and Religion in Current Art." *New Art Examiner* 12 (January 1985): 53.

Klein, Ellen Lee. "Square and…" *Arts Magazine* 61:6 (February 1987): 108-9.

Lyon, Christopher. "Painters Take Two Views of Realism." *Chicago Sun-Times*, 15 April 1984.

——— . "Spiritual Subjects Change Form." *Chicago Sun-Times*, 19 October 1984.

McCracken, David. "Hollywood Makes an Impression on Artist." *Chicago Tribune*, 3 November 1989.

Raynor, Vivian. "Bennington to Bronx: Canvases Span the Gap." *New York Times*, 10 February 1991.

Upshaw, Regan. "Anne Abrons at Ruth Siegel." *Art in America* 73:6 (June 1985): 143.

Westfall, Stephen. "Anne Abrons." *Arts Magazine* 59:8 (April 1985): 41.

——— . "Ten Variations on a Theme." *Arts Magazine* 57:2 (October 1982): 10.

Selected Collections

Becton Dickson and Company

John D. and Catherine T. MacArthur Foundation, Chicago

Greater Lafayette Museum of Art, Lafayette, Indiana

Keith Hartley, Edinburgh

Madison Art Center, Wisconsin

Museum of Contemporary Art, Chicago

Neuberger and Berman, New York

Neuberger Museum, State University of New York, Purchase

Rayovac Corporation, Madison, Wisconsin

Western Electric Corporation

TIM DOUD

Born New Bedford, Massachusetts, 1961
M.F.A., School of the Art Institute
  of Chicago, 1992
Skowhegan School of Painting and
  Sculpture, Maine, 1992
B.S., Columbia College, Missouri, 1984

Exhibition Checklist

9. *Halstead*, 1993
   Oil on linen
   30 x 36 in. (76.2 x 91.4 cm)
   Courtesy of the artist

10. *Halstead (Studio Blanket)*, 1994
    Oil on linen
    30 x 36 in. (76.2 x 91.4 cm)
    Courtesy of the artist

11. *Bishop Frank Griswold*, 1994-95
    Oil on linen
    60 x 36 in. (152.4 x 91.4 cm)
    Lent by the Episcopal Diocese of Chicago

12. *Halstead (Portrait II)*, 1994-95
    Oil on linen
    40 x 40 in. (101.6 x 101.6 cm)
    Courtesy of the artist

13. *Francisco St. (CK)*, 1995
    Oil on linen
    30 x 30 in. (76.2 x 76.2 cm)
    Courtesy of the artist

14. *Francisco St. (CKII)*, 1995
    Oil on linen
    30 x 30 in. (76.2 x 76.2 cm)
    Courtesy of the artist

15. *Giulietta*, 1995
    Oil on linen
    72 x 40 in. (182.9 x 101.6 cm)
    Courtesy of the artist

Selected Group Exhibitions

1995

Go Figure, Black and Greenberg Gallery,
New York

Tim Doud, Brent Gearan, Frank Trankina,
Hyde Park Art Center, Chicago

1994

The Shape of Things, Contemporary Art
Workshop, Chicago

Toybomb!, Hyde Park Art Center, Chicago
Judith Racht Gallery, Harbert, Michigan

Evanston and Vicinity 12th Biennial Exhibition,
Evanston Art Center, Illinois

Tim Doud, Brent Gearan, Frank Trankina,
Artemisia Gallery, Chicago

1993

Hyde Park Art Center, Chicago

Tim Doud, Brent Gearan, and Frank Trankina,
Contemporary Art Workshop, Chicago

1992

Tim Doud, Brent Gearan, and Frank Trankina,
Prairie Avenue Gallery, Chicago

CAA/MFA, Gallery 2, School of the Art
Institute of Chicago

Body and Soul, Warren Street Gallery,
Hudson, New York

Qu'Art, Beret International Gallery, Chicago

Anonymous Museum, Chicago

*Next Generation: The Impact of Race and Sexuality
on Family Life*, Gallery 2, School of the Art
Institute of Chicago

1990

Bay Arts 90, San Mateo Arts Council,
California

1989

Art against AIDS, Wexner Center for the Arts,
Ohio State University, Columbus

The Subject Is AIDS, Nexus Contemporary Art
Center, Atlanta

OCCCA Annual Exhibit, Orange County
Center for Contemporary Art, Santa Ana

1988

Art Addressing AIDS, San Francisco State
University Art Gallery

Cal Works, Cal Expo, Sacramento

Bearing Witness: Artists Respond to AIDS, Mobius
Gallery, Boston and Hera Educational
Foundation, Wakefield, Rhode Island

1987

Look at Me!, Works Gallery, San Jose

Art and Well Being...Living with the Epidemic,
New Langton Arts and Colorbox Gallery,
San Francisco

Bibliography

Anderson, Larry Jens, Dan Tally,
et al. *The Subject Is AIDS*. Atlanta:
Nexus Contemporary Art Center, 1989.

Artner, Alan. "The Plague Years."
Chicago Tribune, 1 November 1992.

Curamoto, Susan. "Mural Painters
Experience Adorning Area Walls."
Columbia Missourian, 29 April 1983.

Demos, T. "Tim Doud, Brent Gearan,
and Frank Trankina [at] Contemporary Art
Workshop." *New Art Examiner* 20:9 (May
1993): 41-42.

Evans, Paul. "The Subject Is AIDS."
Art Papers 3:2 (March/April 1989): 45-46.

Fox, Catherine. "The Subject Is AIDS."
Atlanta Journal and Constitution, 13 January 1989.

Hartness, Ruth. "AIDS as Primary Concern."
Creative Loafing [Atlanta], January 1989.

Holtz, Sigrid. "Local Artist Finds
Portraits a Good Start for His Career."
Columbia Missourian, 8 July 1983.

Norklun, Kathi. "Many Feminisms."
Woodstock Times, 22 October 1992.

Rodriguez, Johnette. "Artists on AIDS."
The New Paper [Providence], 25 May–
2 June 1988.

Sullivan, Carl. "Art/AIDS." *Art and Performance*
[Evanston, Illinois], 6 November 1992.

White, Valerie. "Body and Souls of All
Women's Lives Confront Viewers at
Exhibit." *Register-Star* [Hudson, New York],
13 October 1992.

Selected Collections

Marie and Robert Bergman, Chicago

David Brunetti, San Francisco

Robert S. Cohn, Chicago

Edward Dickson, Chicago

Episcopal Diocese of Chicago

Denise and Stephen F. Doctor, Chicago

John Easton and Sem Sutter, Chicago

Barry Finklestein and Stephanie Wynn,
    Highland Park, Illinois

Gregory G. Knight, Chicago

Joan Livingstone, Chicago

Donald and Marcia McInerney,
    Deerfield, Illinois

Thomas Mohan, New York

Mark and Nancy Palmer,
    Highland Park, Illinois

Georgie and Jerry Suttin, Deerfield, Illinois

Ray Yoshida, Chicago

Young and Rubicon Art Agency,
    Copenhagen

DAN GUSTIN

Born San Francisco, 1948
M.F.A., School of Art and Architecture,
  Yale University, New Haven,
  Connecticut, 1974
B.F.A., Kansas City Art Institute,
  Missouri, 1972
Yale Summer School at Norfolk,
  Connecticut, 1970
Cal-Western University, San Diego, 1969

Exhibition Checklist

16. *First Scene*, 1993-95
  Oil on canvas
  96 x 72 in. (243.9 x 182.9 cm)
  Courtesy of the artist

17. *Untitled*, 1994-95
  Acrylic on canvas
  96 x 144 in. (243.9 x 365.8 cm)
  Lent by David Dallison, Chicago

Individual Exhibitions

1995
Dan Gustin: Heroic-Scale Works, Rockford Art
Museum, Illinois

1994
Lyons Wier Gallery, Chicago

1992
Lloyd Shin Gallery, Chicago

1991
Bowery Gallery, New York

1988, 1987, 1986, 1985
J. Rosenthal Gallery, Chicago

1982, 1980
Alpha Gallery, Boston

1979
Munson Gallery, New Haven, Connecticut

1978
Forum Gallery, New York

1977
Alpha Gallery, Boston

1976
Paul Mellon Arts Center, Wallingford,
Connecticut

Selected Group Exhibitions

1995
The Expressionist Narrative: Storytellers,
UWM Art Museum, University of
Wisconsin at Milwaukee

1994, 1993
Lyons Wier Gallery, Chicago

1992
Painters Who Teach, J. Rosenthal Gallery,
Chicago

1991
Spirited Visions: Portraits of Chicago Artists,
State of Illinois Gallery, Chicago

1990
Bowery Gallery, New York

29 Chicago Artists, Spurgeon Gallery, Central
Washington University, Ellensburg,
Washington

1989
J. Rosenthal Gallery, Chicago

Struve Gallery, Chicago

Yale at Chicago, Gallery Vienna, Chicago

Chicago at Terre Haute, Indiana State
University, Terre Haute

New to New York, Marilyn Pearl Gallery,
New York

J. Rosenthal Gallery, Chicago

Masquerade, Randolph Street Gallery, Chicago

1987

Kyrgier/Landau Gallery, Los Angeles

Contemporary American Drawing, Fine Arts Gallery, University of Indiana, Bloomington

1986

Chicago Artists, Carol Rubiner Gallery, Detroit

Self-Portraits Then or Now, ARC Gallery, Chicago

Couples 11, Suburban Fine Arts Center, Arlington Heights, Illinois

1985

Selected Alumni, Kansas City Art Institute, Missouri

5" x 5", N.A.M.E. Gallery, Chicago

American Drawing, J. Rosenthal Gallery, Chicago

Midwest Realists, Paine Art Center and Arboretum, Oshkosh, Wisconsin

1984

J. Rosenthal Gallery, Chicago

Five by Five, Frumkin and Struve Gallery, Chicago

Artists Working in Pilsen, Northern Illinois University, DeKalb

1982

YMCA, New Haven, Connecticut

Munson Gallery, New Haven, Connecticut

Self-Portraits, Alpha Gallery, Boston

1981

Forum Gallery, New York

Urban Landscapes, Queens Gallery, New York

1980

Alpha Gallery, Boston

1979

New England Drawing Competition, DeCordova Museum, Lincoln, Massachusetts

Bibliography

Adrian, Dennis. "Two Decades of Painting in Chicago." *New Art Examiner* 15:4 (December 1987): 26-29.

Artner, Alan. "Dan Gustin at J. Rosenthal." *Chicago Tribune*, 3 November 1986.

Bracalante, Anita. "Chicago Artists Shine at Fine Arts Gallery." *Indianapolis Sunday Herald Times*, 28 October 1987.

Carroll, Patty and James Yood. *Spirited Visions: Portraits of Chicago Artists*. Chicago: University of Chicago Press, 1991.

Davidson, Jalane and Richard. *Midwest Realists*. Oshkosh, Wisconsin: Paine Art Center and Arboretum, 1985.

Dunning, William. "Chicago Art at Spurgeon Gallery." *Observer* [Ellensburg, Washington], 8 March 1990.

Hanson, Henry. "Dan Gustin's Dream-World Paintings at Rosenthal." *Chicago Magazine* 35:10 (November 1986): 100.

Kosidowski, Paul. "The Truth in Painting." In *The Expressionist Narrative: Storytellers*. Milwaukee: UWM Art Museum, 1995.

Paine, Janice. " 'Storytellers,' A Riot of Color." *Milwaukee Sentinel*, 20 February 1995.

Westerbeck, Colin. "Dan Gustin." *Artforum* 25:6 (February 1987): 122-23.

Selected Collections

Art Institute of Chicago

Ron and Meta Berger, Chicago

Leonard Bocour, New York

Buffalo College Museum, New York

David Dallison, Chicago

Richard and Jalane Davidson, Chicago

Bella Fishko, New York

Norbert Gleicher, Chicago

Hirshhorn Museum and Sculpture Garden, Washington, D.C.

Miller Drawing Collection, New York

Rockford Art Museum, Illinois

Worcester Art Museum, Massachusetts

MARK JACKSON

Born Harrisburg, Illinois, 1952
B.F.A., School of the Art Institute
  of Chicago, 1977
San Francisco Art Institute, 1973-74

Exhibition Checklist

18. *Untitled (Seated Nude)*, 1992
    Oil on canvas
    40 x 32 in. (101.6 x 81.2 cm)
    Courtesy of the artist

19. *Self-Portrait*, 1993
    Oil on canvas
    20 x 16 in. (50.8 x 40.6 cm)
    Courtesy of the artist

20. *Untitled*, 1993
    Oil on canvas
    34 x 56 in. (86.4 x 142.2 cm)
    Courtesy of the artist

21. *Untitled*, 1993
    Oil on canvas
    20 x 26 in. (50.8 x 66.0 cm)
    Courtesy of the artist

22. *Self-Portrait*, 1994
    Oil on canvas
    20 x 26 in. (50.8 x 66.0 cm)
    Courtesy of the artist

23. *Standing Nude*, 1995
    Oil on canvas
    72 x 48 in. (182.9 x 121.9 cm)
    Courtesy of the artist

Individual Exhibitions

1992

Judith Racht Gallery, Harbert, Michigan

1990

Printworks, Chicago

1987

Union League Club of Chicago

Betsy Rosenfield Gallery, Chicago

Gallery 210, University of Missouri,
St. Louis

1986, 1984, 1982

Betsy Rosenfield Gallery, Chicago

Selected Group Exhibitions

1992

Face to Face: Self-Portraits by Chicago Artists,
Chicago Cultural Center

1991

New Acquisitions: The MCA Collects, Museum
of Contemporary Art, Chicago

1990

Personal/Political: Sexuality Self-Defined, Gallery
2, School of the Art Institute of Chicago

1989

Decay: A Tribute to Ivan Albright, Ukrainian
Institute of Modern Art, Chicago

*16th Union League Club Art Competition and
Exhibition*, Union League Club of Chicago
(first prize)

1988

The Flower Show, Betsy Rosenfield Gallery,
Chicago

*The Developing Image: Continuity and Change
in a Chicago Artistic Tradition*, University Art
Museum, University of New Mexico,
Albuquerque

1987

Masks by Chicago Artists, Klein Gallery, Chicago

*15th Union League Club Art Competition and
Exhibition*, Union League Club of Chicago
(third prize)

1986

81st Exhibition by Artists of Chicago and Vicinity,
Art Institute of Chicago

Chicago Draws, Hyde Park Art Center,
Chicago

*The Contemporary Arts Center Biennial,
Contemporary Arts Center*, Cincinnati (traveled
to Cleveland Institute of Art, and Herron
Gallery, Indianapolis Center for
Contemporary Art through 1987)

*Artist/Source: Influence, Stimuli, Inspiration,
Obsession*, Gallery 200, School of Art,
Northern Illinois University, DeKalb
(traveled to School of the Art Institute
Gallery, Chicago; and Art and Architecture
Gallery, University of Tennessee, Knoxville
through 1987)

1985

Then and Now, Hyde Park Art Center,
Chicago

Looking at Men, Artemisia Gallery, Chicago

*14th Union League Club Art Competition and
Exhibition*, Union League Club of Chicago
(first prize)

1984

80th Exhibition by Artists of Chicago and Vicinity,
Art Institute of Chicago (Logan Prize)

Painting and Sculpture Today 1984, Indianapolis
Museum of Art

*Joseph Yoakum: His Influence on Contemporary Art
and Artists*, Carl Hammer Gallery, Chicago

1983

*19th Bradley National Print and Drawing
Exhibition*, Lakeview Museum, Peoria, Illinois
(traveled)

Looking at Women, Artemisia Gallery, Chicago

1982

*The Big Pitcher: 20 Years of the Abstracted Figure in
Chicago Art*, Hyde Park Art Center, Chicago

1981

78th Exhibition by Artists of Chicago and Vicinity,
Art Institute of Chicago

Bibliography

Adrian, Dennis. "Mark Jackson."
Arts Magazine 56:9 (May 1982): 22.

Artner, Alan. "Mark Jackson." *Chicago Tribune*,
9 March 1990.

Bonesteel, Michael. "Mark Jackson."
Artforum 23:3 (November 1984): 107.

Cameron, Dan. "A New Generation of
Chicago Artists." *Art News* 83:8 (October
1984): 110.

Delacoma, Wynne. "Gallery Cultivates
New Exhibitors for Flower Show."
Chicago Sun-Times, 15 January 1988.

Frueh, Joanna. "Mark Jackson at
Betsy Rosenfield." *Art in America* 74:11
(November 1986): 175, 177.

Hixson, Kathryn. "On Exhibit:
A Gallery Full of Flowers."
Chicago Reader, 15 January 1988.

Kuspit, Donald. "The Madness of Chicago
Art." *New Art Examiner* 13 (May 1986): 22-26.

Lyon, Christopher. "Coming in from the
Cold." *Chicago Magazine* 33:5 (May 1984): 156.

——— . "Hyde Park Show Fuels Interest
in Figurative Art." *Chicago Sun-Times*,
30 January 1983.

Mills, Dan. "Mark Jackson." In *Artist/Source:
Influence, Stimuli, Inspiration, Obsession*. DeKalb,
Illinois: Northern Illinois University, 1986.

Vine, Naomi. "Strength of Conviction:
Mark Jackson's Paintings." *Arts Magazine* 58:9
(May 1984): 138.

Vine, Richard. "Mark Jackson: Blood
Phobia." *Dialogue* 11:3 (May/June 1988): 18.

Selected Collections

Arkansas Arts Center, Little Rock

Evelyn and Larry Aronson, Glencoe, Illinois

Mrs. Edwin Bergman, Chicago

Big Chicks/Michelle Fire Collection,
Chicago

Dr. and Mrs. Peter Broido,
West Chicago, Illinois

Dr. Thomas Carlson, Chicago

Achim Davis, Paris

First National Bank of Chicago

Ruth Horwich, Chicago

Jones/Faulkner Collection, Chicago

Monique Knowlton, New York

Museum of Contemporary Art, Chicago

Gerald Nordland and Paula Giannini,
Chicago

David and Alfred Smart Museum of Art,
University of Chicago

Donna and Howard Stone, Chicago

ROBERT LUCY

Born Camp Lejeune, N.C., 1965
M.F.A., School of the Art Institute
of Chicago, 1990
B.F.A., School of the Art Institute
of Chicago, 1988
Northwestern University, Evanston,
Illinois, 1984-86

Exhibition Checklist

24. *Reclining Nude with Flowers*, 1992
Oil on linen
48 x 60 in. (121.9 x 152.4 cm)
Lent by Mrs. Bernadette Komenda,
Justice, Illinois

25. *Artist and Models*, 1993
Oil on linen
78 x 60 in. (198.1 x 152.4 cm)
Lent by Rolf Achilles, Chicago

26. *Laura with Hats*, 1993
Oil on linen
46 x 36 in. (116.8 x 91.4 cm)
Lent by Mr. and Mrs. Howard Tullman,
Chicago

27. *Stephanie D'Alessandro and David Rownd*, 1993
Oil on linen
48 x 56 in. (121.9 x 142.2 cm)
Lent by Stephanie D'Alessandro and
David Rownd, Chicago

28. *The Mesmerist*, 1994
Oil on linen
48 x 36 in. (121.9 x 91.4 cm)
Lent by Michael Stavy, Chicago

29. *Portrait of Sylvia Sleigh*, 1995
Oil on canvas
72 x 36 in. (182.9 x 91.4 cm)
Lent by Sylvia Sleigh, New York

30. *Self-Portrait*, 1995
Oil on linen
35 x 35 in. (88.9 x 88.9 cm)
Courtesy of Sonia Zaks Gallery, Chicago

Individual Exhibitions

1994
Zaks Gallery, Chicago

Selected Group Exhibitions

1994
The Human Condition, Greater Lafayette
Museum of Art, Lafayette, Indiana

1993
Party Mix, Hyde Park Art Center, Chicago
Aquatic Visions, John G. Shedd Aquarium,
Chicago

1992
Flora 92, Chicago Botanic Garden
Face to Face: Self-Portraits by Chicago Artists,
Chicago Cultural Center

1991
Union League Club of Chicago

1989
New Still Life, Evanston Art Center, Illinois
Dennis Adrian: A Critical Subject, Struve Gallery,
Chicago

Bibliography

Adrian, Dennis. *New Still Life*. Evanston,
Illinois: Evanston Art Center, 1989.

Bonesteel, Michael. "New Life
for Still Life." *Pioneer Press Newspaper*,
28 September 1989.

Hixson, Kathryn. "New Still Life."
Arts Magazine 64:4 (December 1989): 106.

Holg, Garett. "New Still Life [at] Evanston
Art Center." *New Art Examiner* 17:5 (January
1990): 41-42.

McCracken, David. "Hollywood Makes
an Impression on Artist." *Chicago Tribune*,
3 November 1989.

Selected Collections

Anne Abrons and David Sharpe, New York

Rolf Achilles, Chicago

John Baum and Laura Satersmoen,
    San Francisco

Marie and Robert Bergman, Chicago

Richard Born, Chicago

Wayne Comper, Sydney

Stephanie D'Alessandro and David Rownd,
    Chicago

George Danforth, Chicago

Edward Dickson, Chicago

Denise and Stephen F. Doctor, Chicago

Nancy Ganiard and Kevin Smith, Chicago

Mr. and Mrs. Larry Gerber, Highland Park

Mr. and Mrs. Nathan Grossman,
    Deerfield, Illinois

Drs. Kay and Patrick Haney, Clearwater,
    Florida

Keith Hartley, Edinburgh

Peter Hawrylewicz and Ken Lieber,
    Miami Beach, Florida

Patricia John, Chicago

Dr. and Mrs. James Jones, Chicago

Jones/Faulkner Collection, Chicago

Mrs. Bernadette Komenda, Justice, Illinois

Deeann Levy, Chicago

Paul LaMantia, Chicago

Bernard and Ruth Nath,
    Highland Park, Illinois

Kenneth Northcott, Chicago

Mark Pollack, Chicago

Linda Sandell and David Schwartz, Seattle

Sylvia Sleigh, New York

Michael Stavy, Chicago

Mr. and Mrs. Steve Stern, Chicago

Donna and Howard Stone, Chicago

Lolli Thurm, Chicago

Mr. and Mrs. Howard A. Tullman, Chicago

Timothy Wittman, Chicago

RICHARD WILLENBRINK

Born Louisville, Kentucky, 1954

M.F.A., Northern Illinois University,
DeKalb, 1979

B.F.A., University of Notre Dame,
South Bend, Indiana, 1976

Exhibition Checklist

31. *Nude with a Knife*, 1991
Oil on linen
48 x 54 in. (121.9 x 137.2 cm)
Lent by Deeann Levy, Chicago

32. *Salome*, 1992
Oil on linen
54 x 70 in. (137.2 x 177.8 cm)
Lent by Donna and Howard Stone,
Chicago

33. *The Flaying of Marsyas*, 1993
Oil on linen
72 x 72 in. (182.9 x 182.9 cm)
Lent by Patricia John, Chicago

34. *Orchidelirium*, 1993
Oil on linen
52 x 64 in. (132.1 x 162.6 cm)
Lent by Marjorie and Herbert Friedman,
Riverwoods, Illinois

35. *Nude Self-Portrait*, 1995
Oil on linen
74 x 44 in. (188.0 x 111.8 cm)
Courtesy of Sonia Zaks Gallery, Chicago

36. *Seated Model in the Studio*, 1995
Oil on canvas
60 x 60 in. (152.4 x 152.4 cm)
Courtesy of Sonia Zaks Gallery, Chicago

37. *Self-Portrait in a Red Robe*, 1995
Oil on linen
44 x 28 in. (111.8 x 71.1 cm)
Courtesy of Sonia Zaks Gallery, Chicago

Individual Exhibitions

1993

Zaks Gallery, Chicago

Selected Group Exhibitions

1995

*Flora: Contemporary Artists and
the World of Flowers*, Leigh Yawkey Woodson
Art Museum, Wausau, Wisconsin (traveled
to Art Museum of Southeast Texas,
Beaumont; New Mexico Museum of
Natural History and Science, Albuquerque;
Gibbes Museum of Art, Charleston, South
Carolina; Dixon Gallery and Gardens,
Memphis through 1996)

1994

Just Good Art, Hyde Park Art Center, Chicago

1993

Six Painters, Hyde Park Art Center, Chicago

1992

Flora 92, Chicago Botanic Garden

Face to Face: Self-Portraits by Chicago Artists,
Chicago Cultural Center

1991

*Realism, Figurative Painting, and the Chicago
Viewpoint: Selections from the Permanent Collection*,
Museum of Contemporary Art, Chicago

1989

New Still Life, Evanston Art Center, Illinois

Dennis Adrian: A Critical Subject, Struve Gallery,
Chicago

Northern Illinois University Gallery,
Chicago

Union League Club, Chicago

1988

Madonna and Child, St. Patrick's Church and
Zolla Lieberman Gallery, Chicago

1987

The Flower Show, Betsy Rosenfield Gallery,
Chicago

Figure Painting in Chicago, Northern Illinois
University, DeKalb

1986

Portraits from the Permanent Collection,
Museum of Contemporary Art, Chicago

Chicago Painters, Krannert Art Museum,
University of Illinois at Urbana-Champaign

1985

Then and Now, Hyde Park Center, Chicago

1984

Observations: Four Realist Painters,
N.A.M.E. Gallery, Chicago

80th Exhibition by Artists of Chicago and Vicinity,
Art Institute of Chicago

1983

Chicago: Some Other Traditions, Madison Art Center, Wisconsin (traveled to Sheldon Memorial Art Gallery, University of Nebraska, Lincoln; Norman MacKensie Art Gallery, University of Regina, Saskatchewan; Sarah Campbell Blaffer Art Gallery, University of Houston; Loch Haven Art Center, Orlando; Anchorage Historical and Fine Arts Museum; Arkansas Art Center, Little Rock through 1986)

Emerging Artists, Renaissance Society at the University of Chicago

Bibliography

Adrian, Dennis. *New Still Life*. Evanston, Illinois: Evanston Art Center, 1989.

————. "Richard Willenbrink." In *Chicago: Some Other Traditions*. Madison, Wisconsin: Madison Art Center, 1983.

Artner, Alan. "Realists Repeat History to Distraction." *Chicago Tribune*, 30 March 1984.

Bonesteel, Michael. "New Life for Still Life." *Pioneer Press Newspaper*, 28 September 1989.

Garver, Thomas H. "Flowers and the Spheres of Life: Some Personal Thoughts about Artists and Flowers" and "Richard Willenbrink." In *Flora: Contemporary Artists and the World of Flowers*. Wausau, Wisconsin: Leigh Yawkey Woodson Art Museum, 1995.

Hanson, Henry. "Artworks." *Chicago Magazine* 40:1 (January 1991): 17-19.

————. "Discovering a Painter in Pilsen." *Chicago Magazine* 32:5 (May 1983): 114.

————. "Go Figure." *Chicago Magazine* 42:4 (April 1993): 16.

Hixson, Kathryn. "New Still Life." *Arts Magazine* 64:4 (December 1989): 105-6.

Holg, Garrett. "New Still Life [at] Evanston Art Center." *New Art Examiner*, 17:5 (January 1990): 41-42.

Holg, Garrett. "Self-Portrait Chicago." *Chicago Sun-Times*, 23 February 1992.

Leonhart, Mark Michael. "Observations: Four Realist Painters." *New Art Examiner* 11:10 (September 1984): 16.

McCracken, David. "Hollywood Makes an Impression on Artist." *Chicago Tribune*, 3 November 1989.

Selected Collections

James Adkins, Chicago

Mr. and Mrs. Henry Buchbinder, Chicago

Edward Dickson, Chicago

Denise and Stephen F. Doctor, Chicago

Marjorie and Herbert Friedman, Riverwoods, Illinois

Mr. and Mrs. Larry Gerber, Highland Park, Illinois

Reverend Andrew Greeley, Chicago

Keith Hartley, Edinburgh, Scotland

Peter Hawrylewicz and Ken Lieber, Miami Beach, Florida

Ruth Horwich, Chicago

Patricia John, Chicago

Jones/Faulkner Collection, Chicago

Kelly Library, Chicago

Deeann Levy, Chicago

Kenneth Northcott, Chicago

Mark Pollack, Chicago

Rayovac Corporation, Madison, Wisconsin

David Schwartz and Linda Sandell, Seattle

Linda Sandell, Seattle

David and Alfred Smart Museum of Art, University of Chicago

Donna and Howard Stone, Chicago

Union League Club of Chicago

Michelle Vishny, Chicago

86

PHOTO CREDITS

Peter Accettola
Catalogue number: 29

Tim Doud
Catalogue number: 11

Dan Gustin
Catalogue numbers: 16, 17

David Sharpe
Catalogue numbers: 1, 2, 3, 4, 5, 6, 7, 8

Michael Tropea
Catalogue numbers: 9, 10, 12, 13, 14, 15, 18, 19, 20, 21, 22, 23, 24, 25, 26, 27, 28, 30, 31, 32, 33, 35, 36, 37

Tom Van Eynde
Catalogue numbers: 6, 34

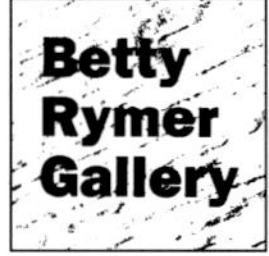

The Betty Rymer Gallery
280 South Columbus Drive
Chicago, Illinois 60603-3103
312.899.5100
312.899.5110 fax